Memoirs of Sir H. L. Playfair, etc.

Sir Hugh Lyon Playfair

Memoirs of Sir H. L. Playfair, etc.
Playfair, Sir Hugh Lyon
British Library, Historical Print Editions
British Library
1861.
8°.
10370.bbb.27.

MEMOIRS

OF

Sir Hugh Lyon Playfair, LL.D., J.P., &c.,

K

LIEUTENANT-COLONEL BENGAL ARTILLERY,

PROVOST OF ST ANDREWS,

AND

HONORARY CUSTODIER OF CROWN PROPERTY

IN THE CITY.

ST ANDREWS: M. FLETCHER.

MDCCCLXI.

P. THOMSON, PRINTER, ST ANDREWS.

INTRODUCTION.

WE offer no apology for presenting the public with the following biographical sketch. Men of the peculiar stamp of Sir HUGH LYON PLAYFAIR are so rare that their lives cannot fail to excite our interest. Although we do not claim for him the title of philosopher, poet, or man of science, no one will deny that he possesses genius. It is as a Social Reformer that we hold him up for imitation, as well as instruction. His whole career has been a continued warfare against moral and physical stagnation. The process began in India, in 1807, to the great astonishment of the station at Bareilly, and is still in active operation in St Andrews in 1860. In carrying out his improvements, indomitable energy, sound judgment, consummate tact and ability, are ever conspicuous. No difficulties are too great to be surmounted ; no opposition too formidable to be overcome ; nothing is beyond the reach of his reforming genius. Streets, houses, schools, libraries, universities, are all indebted to him : while his improvements in municipal administration, and his advancement of the cause of education, chiefly in connection with the Madras College, give him a lasting claim to the gratitude, not only of St Andrews, but of the whole country. His history points him out as one of the remarkable men of this age, and shews how much good may be effected by one man in the amelioration of the social sphere in which he may be placed.

We should not fully accomplish our task, if we overlooked

the taste displayed by Sir Hugh in his many improvements; if we did not notice his gentlemanly bearing, his wit and humour, his high sense of honour, and all those amiable qualities which enchain the affections of his friends, and endear him to every member of his family circle. A patron of learning, he is ever ready to assist and encourage talent. Devoted to music, he has done much to advance its cultivation in the community over which he presides, and the organ in the Madras College is an eminent example of the practical manner in which he gives effect to his ideas.

Many notices have from time to time appeared of what may not inappropriately be termed the resurrection of St Andrews by Sir H. L. Playfair, since the time he entered upon his Provostship in 1842. No attempt, however, has yet been made to give his full career. Our narrative merely proposes to give a sketch of his early life, with an enumeration of the many improvements he has effected in St Andrews. It was suggested by the announcement, that our respected Provost had resigned the office which he had so ably filled for eighteen years; and is chiefly intended to show how consistent has been his character from first to last, and how faithfully he has fulfilled his mission as a Reformer, both in the capacity of a military officer and in that of a civic ruler. In compiling it we have taken advantage of all that has been already written upon the subject, and have endeavoured to supplement by information from other sources. If we owe an apology to any one for its appearance, it is to Sir Hugh himself, whose aid or sanction in the matter has not been obtained, and whose career must in consequence be but imperfectly represented.

Lieutenant-Colonel Sir Hugh Lyon Playfair, LL.D., was born at Meigle on the 17th November 1786. He was educated at that place and at Newtyle, and afterwards at the Grammar School of Dundee. He completed his academic training at the University of St Andrews, where his father Dr Playfair, a member of the Royal Society, and author of a "System of Chrono-logy," was Principal, being previously Historiographer to the Prince of Wales. That he was an ardent student in those years is evident; for after having, in 1804, served a short time in the Volunteers, and being placed on the Colonel's staff, he qualified himself in three months under Professor Playfair of Edinburgh, and Mr Jardine, his tutor, to enter at Woolwich. There he was placed under Dr Hutton and Mr Landman, whose exami-nations he passed successfully in the beginning of 1805.

In March of that year he sailed from Portsmouth, and arrived at Calcutta in August following, where, with characteristic en-ergy, he immediately began to study his profession in all its branches. In 1806, he was selected by the General to command a detachment of European Artillery proceeding to the Upper Provinces; and on this occasion he won golden opinions from his superior officer by conducting his soldiers to Cawnpore, a distance of 800 miles, without having had to punish one of them, and without the loss of a single man.

It is clear that, even at this early period of his career, he must have had the determined will, the uprightness of character, and the kindly bearing to inferiors, which mark the men born to command. Nor were his merits overlooked; for, in a short time, Sir John Horsford appointed him to the command of the Artillery at Bareilly. Had Sir Hugh been a man of feeble or ordinary character, Bareilly, at that time, would have been no proper sphere for him. Great abuses had crept into the depart-ment over which he had command: and when he reached the station he found that the cattle were lent out to the civilians, as well as to an officer high in rank, while the artillerymen were idle and without discipline. Nothing daunted, the youthful artillery officer called in the horses, and refused to allow one to quit the sheds. Great must have been the consternation, and deep the disgust excited by these innovations upon indolence and neglect of duty; but the young reformer proceeded on his course without fear or favour. With a self-denial, which is worthy of the admiration of all men, he restricted his expenses to five pounds per month, in order to rid himself of debt. Eschewing all company, and drilling his detachment twice a-day, he soon brought it to such a state of perfection, that his guns kept up with the cavalry when he was ordered to put down a disturbance in Oude, caused by a robber chief named Tumon Sing, an enterprise in which he was completely successful.

In the year 1807, the fortress of Kumonah being besieged, he volunteered to relinquish his command and proceed to the scene of action. His offer was at first accepted; but it was afterwards countermanded, with many expressions of regard. He was recommended to be appointed to the Horse-Artillery at Agra; and here he spent the year 1808 in constant drill and practice. In January 1809, Sir Hugh marched to join the army at Saharunpore, under General St Leger and General Gillespie. In the following month he reached Sirhind and Lascarrie, and was engaged in frequent skirmishes with the Sikhs. Being about this time selected to go to the fair at Hurdwar to purchase horses, he refused to take any share of them unless he was allowed his choice of them for the Horse-Artillery, as those engaged in that arm of the service did double work. He thus established a principle which has ever since been acted on in the Indian service.

In the end of the same year he was appointed, under peculiarly pleasing circumstances, to the office of Adjutant and Quarter-master to the increased corps of Horse Artillery. The Commander-in-chief had instructed Sir John Horsford to nominate *the most fit in the whole regiment, whomsoever he might be;* and the Adjutant-General, in his public letter, stated that, *in this case, private interest must be sacrificed to public benefit.* Here we cannot but remark, that it would be well for Britain and the interests of civilization, if such sacrifices were more the rule and less the exception. In 1811, Sir Hugh's corps was ordered to be permanently cantoned at Meerut, where he spent two years in bringing his men to a very high state of discipline and efficiency. The reward of his labours was at hand. Towards the close of 1814, General Gillespie, with a large force, attacked the hill fort of Kalunga; and in an attempt to carry it by assault, his men were repulsed with great slaughter. With the impetuosity that marked this brave but unfortunate general, he declared that he would take the fort or lose his life. He kept his word. Far in advance of his men, and cheering them on to the attack, the brave old man fell, shot through the heart.

The attempt to storm the fort having failed, it was resolved to try the effect of artillery. Playfair was accordingly sent for, and he and Major Brookes opened fire with their 18-pounders at 180 yards distance. It was not, however, till four days had passed, that the enemy evacuated the place. During the siege, Sir Hugh was struck by a spent ball on the breast, and his cheek was grazed by the splinter of a shell which exploded in the battery. The attempt to carry the fort by assault cost the British about 800 men in killed and wounded—a loss which would evidently have been avoided had the Artillery been at first brought into operation.

In 1815, Sir Hugh, having recovered from the wounds received at Kalunga, marched to Delhi, Purputgunge, and other places, with Sir William Keir's field force. But severe labour, unremitting study, and the trying climate of the East, began to tell on the health of this athletic soldier. Having been promoted to be Captain of the Horse Artillery, he applied for and obtained furlough to Europe. On this occasion his commanding officer, Colonel Pennington, wrote him regretting as a personal loss the absence of his indefatigable Adjutant, and remarking the unfavourable change which had taken place on the men since he left them. Sir Hugh's life has clearly been continuous, not fragmentary. The youth who landed at Calcutta in 1805 had the same principles as the Artillery Officer of Bareilly, Kalunga, and Dumdum; the same as the man who has devoted

many long years to the sanitary improvement and the embel-
lishment of St Andrews. With a strong but loving hand, he
repressed the excesses of his men, and directed their minds from
vicious courses to manly amusements and virtuous pleasures.
He was, in truth, a Social Reformer of the right stamp; but
you can no more expect an unbroken line of such men in any
office, than you can prove the descent of Pio Nono from the
Apostle Peter. No wonder is it, then, that when his guiding
hand was absent, recourse was had to severe measures in order
to preserve discipline.

In June 1817, he sailed from Calcutta; and having touched
at St Helena, spent a day with Madame Bertrand, and saw
Buonaparte. For three years he improved his mind, and enlarged his ideas, by travelling over England, Scotland, Ireland,
France, Belgium, and Holland. In 1820, he was presented
with the freedom of St Andrews, a city which may figuratively
be said to be as deeply indebted to him as Rome was to Augus-
tus, who found it of brick and left it of marble.

On his return to India, after his marriage in the same year,
he was offered the command of a troop of Horse Artillery by the
Marquis of Hastings. This, however, he declined, and applied
for the office of Superintendent of the Great Military Road, Telegraph Towers, and Post-office Department, between Calcutta
and Benares. In this high office, one of the best in the gift of
the Governor-General, his clear-headedness, love of order, per-
sistency of will, and high administrative ability, found a befit-
ting sphere of action. He held this appointment for nearly
seven years, resigning it on his promotion to be Major, and on
his being appointed to command the 4th Battalion of Artillery
at Dumdum. Before demitting his Superintendency, he requested the Government to appoint a committee to report on
the manner in which he had discharged his duties. That committee travelled over the whole road, 440 miles in length, from
Benares to Calcutta, and reported that the Superintendent had

completely implemented his part of the contract; that with him originated the staging bungalows; and that, instead of having the road open by the end of March or April, as had formerly been the case, he had rendered it available to the public by the month of November. After a glowing eulogium on his fitness for the office, the Committee certified his bridges to be efficient, the telegraph towers to be in a state that could not be surpassed; and that in the post-office department his runners proceeded with nearly double the speed of those of the Postmaster-General.

Of his labours at Dumdum, where he resided for the three years previous to resigning his command, the best idea will be formed from the following letter, addressed to him by the Non-commissioned Officers, Privates, and Heads of Departments in the Artillery Regiment stationed at that place :—

To Major H. L. PLAYFAIR.   DUMDUM, 4th July 1831.

SIR,—We, the undersigned, the Committee of Management of the 4th Battalion Library and Reading-Room, and the Performers in the Dumdum Theatre, desire, on your giving over the command of the Battalion, which you have, we beg to say, held with such distinguished honour to yourself and comfort and advantage to ourselves and comrades, to offer you our heart-felt acknowledgements for the uniform and effective support which your patronage has afforded us in our humble attempts to present a rational and pleasing amusement to our patrons and fellow-soldiers, and in establishing and augmenting the institution to which the surplus funds of the Theatre are intended to be appropriated.

It is not merely because your patronage has been valuable to us, or that therefore you justly merit our most grateful thanks, that we now take leave to obtrude on your notice, but that the peculiar merit attached to the conception of the plans formed by you for the moral and intellectual welfare of the men under your command, whether as regards their present value, or the important benefit they are so well calculated still to afford, seems imperiously to call for some decided acknowledgement on our part. It is under these feelings we now venture to address you.

While we thus tender you the meed of gratitude so justly your due, we cannot refrain from expressing our fears of the loss which the Theatre and Library will sustain by being deprived of your countenance and support. We therefore respectfully beg to say, that we should feel very happy and grateful should you think it proper to leave such a recommendation of our little establishments with our present commanding Officer, as may possibly in some degree compensate the loss which we cannot but sustain by your leaving us; and we venture humbly to hope, that you will not think our present request untimely, as we are induced to make it by our earnest desire to do what we can to promote the interests of the establishments which you took such an active interest in forming; and we do earnestly hope that your successor will see the propriety of affording his countenance to institutions which have for their object the rational amusement and intellectual improvement of the men under his command, and which, from their evident tendency to counteract a too general resort to the canteen, cannot but tend, in no trifling degree, to the amelioration of their general habits, and consequently to promote the mutual comfort of officers and men.

But, to return to the main object of our letter, we one and all beg, with feelings of the deepest gratitude and esteem, most respectfully to offer you our warmest thanks for the many acts of kindness and condescension we have experienced from you; and with them our sincere wishes for the health and happiness of your lady, yourself, and family. May you, Sir, experience a safe and pleasant voyage home, and a happy meeting with your friends in "the land of your fathers;" and we venture to express a hope that, even in the happiest moments of social-enjoyment, this humble tribute of gratitude from your faithful servants, with the conviction that it is amply merited on your part, will be a subject of such pleasing recurrence as to afford that truly grateful test which, under such circumstances, cannot fail to be experienced by every *mens conscia recti*.

We have the honour to remain, Sir, your most obedient and very humble servants,

Signed by the Non-commissioned Officers and
Heads of Departments.

The amusements alluded to were the establishment of a Theatre in the Barracks, a Library, Messes in the Regiment, a Fines' Court, the games of Golf, Cricket, and Bowls, and Gymnastics. There was also exercise of the field guns in different parts of the adjacent country, the guns being dismounted, carried piece-meal over ditches and rivulets, remounted, and a prize given to the men who fired the first round. Such amusements and occupations were very popular among the men, and made them active and intelligent soldiers. Crime and drunkenness were almost unknown in the Battalion; and the punishment of small irregularities was, by order of the Major, awarded by a jury of the men themselves. In this system, which was attended with the happiest results, he anticipated, in practice, one of the most important suggestions of a writer in the *Times* upon the reform of the naval and military code.

It is gratifying to observe that his efforts to make his troops better men and more effective soldiers, did not fail to call forth their esteem and affection. We cannot forbear inserting another letter from a higher quarter.

MUSSOOIN, 12th May 1830.

MY DEAR PLAYFAIR,—In the meantime, I wish to know what are your plans, and whether, in the event of my appointment as Commandant of the Artillery in Bengal, you would accept of the appointment of Adjutant-General.

You are the only person to whom I can write with any freedom, or in whom I can place any confidence, or from whom I can receive the information you can so ably afford.

(Signed)   C. BROWN,
General, Artillery.

To Major Playfair, commanding 4th Battalion Artillery, &c.

He had resolved, however, to return to Britain, and previous to his departure he was offered a public dinner by the officers of Artillery, and complimentary orders were issued by the Commandant on his return to Europe.

His promotion to a Lieutenant-Colonelcy, his election to the Provostship of St Andrews, and his Knighthood by Her Majesty, fall to be noticed in the subsequent part of these memoirs; but we cannot conclude this sketch of his earlier life without expressing our conviction, that had his career in India been later by thirty years, his name would have been blazoned on the roll of fame with the Lawrences, the Outrams, and the Havelocks, who have become household words wherever honour, patriotism, and generous valour are esteemed.

PAULA MAJORA CANAMUS.

Let us sing of the Major not little but much,
For I'm sure in broad Scotland you'll scarcely find such.
St Andrews' Provost—the wonderful man—
The plan of whose being is—ever to plan.
Whose caput has always some new scheme a-brewing,
To bring in improvements where all once was ruin;
    You may talk of fine heroes of Greece and of Troy,
    A fig for such boobies—The Major's the boy.

Just look at the pavement, d'ye mind of the old?
Such heights and such hollows, most vile to behold;
But to walk on,—destruction to comfort and ease!
Now all is as fair and as smooth as you please.
The corns of old ladies, surprised at the change,
Are quite happy along the wide plainstones to range;
    Then away with those heroes of Greece and of Troy,
    What are all to the Major? The Major's the boy.

All unsightly projections that block up the way,
The Major whisks off, ere a word you can say;
You see them at night, and you've seen them for years,
But morning comes in, and no outshot appears!
It has vanished away like the dream of the morn,
Leaving poor old Miss ——s like two maidens forlorn.
    Then a fig for your heroes of Greece and of Troy,
    And huzza for the Major—The Major's the boy!

All strait ways he opens, all wide ways he straits,
All forward old walls he takes back with their gates;
He heeds not refusal, remonstrance, or scold;
E'en the Principal's nose he intends to take off. *
All men who wear whiskers, I'd have you to shave 'em;
For by japers it's odds, if the Major don't shave 'em;
    Then away with your heroes of Greece and of Troy,
    And bravo, the Major—The Major's the boy.

So much building up, and so much knocking down,
Was never yet known in an old Scottish town;
The dust flies for ever; but still let it rise,
There's none o't designed for the honest folk's eyes.
Straight forward's the Major, as one of his streets,
And he still has a kind word for each man he meets;
    Then no more of your heroes of Greece and of Troy,
    But all hearts with the Major—The Major's the boy.

* A mysterious allusion to a certain porch once standing near the College Library.

SIR H. L. PLAYFAIR

AND

ST ANDREWS.

AFTER being denuded of its archiepiscopal pre-eminence, St Andrews rapidly sunk into complete and apparently irretrievable decay; and even since the commencement of the present century, when the fragile tenements of timber, which formed a very considerable proportion of the abodes of the citizens, were substituted by erections of stone, much was wanting to effect the renovation of the town, and to secure the comfort of the inhabitants. Still the streets were covered with grass—the watercourses obstructed by mud, and the external aspect of the houses dingy and disagreeable. If reforms were achieved, they were to promote individual interests alone—if general reform was attempted, for want of funds it generally failed. Amid crumbling walls and green-clad streets, the citizens lived in contented ease and hopeless indifference. A golden age was, however, in reserve for the ancient but long neglected metropolis. Lieutenant-Colonel Sir Hugh Lyon Playfair, LL.D., of St Leonards (then holding rank as Major, and under this name carrying out most of the improvements mentioned in the following pages), was elected chief magistrate of the burgh on the 4th November 1842, and from this date we must trace that course of reform which has renovated the town into a worthy remnant of its bygone splendour.

For many years previous to Sir Hugh's accession to the civic chair, the members of the Town Council were divided into parties; and amid complicated lawsuits, and useless disputations, the funds of the city were consumed. As the first step to reform, the Provost successfully recommended the various contending parties to settle their disputes by arbitration, and to avoid such differences for the future. Having thus promoted union at the council-board, and retrieved the funds of the corporation, Sir Hugh immediately devoted himself to the permanent improvement of the city.

As few towns in the empire stood in greater need of thorough repair and complete renovation, till within the last few years, so we may confidently affirm that few places in the kingdom have, within the same short period, undergone a more sweeping metamorphosis. The principal streets, during the latter months of summer, used to be covered with grass; the common sewers were insufficient, and allowed mud and filth to collect in their courses; the occasional foot pavement along the principal streets was broken and useless; the public buildings and houses of the most respectable citizens were rendered haunted and dismal from the entire absence of external decoration, and scarcely a vestige remained of primitive renown. In North Street, one of the longest and most important of the streets, the eastern portion, inhabited by the fisher population, was the region of putridity and stagnation; while the whole presented

> " —— streetward dunghills festering to the ray
> Of mid-day sun, and causeway that retained
> Of sun-dried fish the glaze."

Sir Hugh L. Playfair resigned the service of the H.E.I.C. on the 10th February 1834, and took up his residence at St Andrews. To spend the evening of his days there had ever been the most ardent desire of his heart; and, indeed, he purchased his present abode before he could return to inhabit it, in order to rivet one link of the chain which was to bind him to the old city during life.

It was on the election of Sir H. L. Playfair to the Provost-ship, in the end of the year 1842, that the state of matters in the city began to undergo a decided change; and from that date may be traced the progress of those repairs, renovations, and improvements in St Andrews, which, associated with Sir Hugh's name, are likely to be long recollected, applauded, and admired. He conceived that it was the duty of a chief magistrate, not merely to attend to the usual routine of burgh affairs, to the discussion of ephemeral political questions, and to the duties of a justice of the peace, but to seek, by every means in his power, the decoration of the city of which he was the highest officer, the encouragement of the inhabitants in the way of honest industry, and, in every respect, the promotion of its interests in comfort, in morals, and religion. Thus impressed, and being connected with the city from early life, and possessing an independent fortune and ample means so far to effect its reformation and carry out his schemes, the Provost first devoted himself to a quiet general survey of the city, that he might detect what was most unseemly, uncomfortable, and incommodious, that these might be first removed, repaired and corrected. The next point was to raise the necessary amount of funds to defray the expense of the projected improvements. This, indeed, was a most important step, and to achieve it required much more than ordinary tact, prudence, and penetration. During the past period of the present century, many would-be improvers of the city had arisen, who had, from time to time, with much taste and care, planned and devised many improvements and renovations, and had obtained estimates of cost, and calculated the general amount required for carrying on operations. But here their labours ceased and their exertions terminated. In vain the most enthusiastic and influential reformer appealed to the feelings of the citizens and surrounding neighbourhood to distend their purse-strings and display their disinterested liberality. While all acknowledged the need of reformation, and approved of plans to produce it, few, if any, would consent to give aid by pecuniary contribution. We believe we are correct in stating that, of the many public-spirited men whom St Andrews has produced during the last half century prior to 1842, and who were eagerly

bent on its improvement, not one of them had influence or eloquence sufficient to induce the inhabitants voluntarily to engage,
by pecuniary aid, in favour of any object merely calculated to
produce comfort and convenience in the city. A respectable-
looking house might occasionally be erected—objects of evident
utility might be from time to time reared by public subscription ;
but aught pertaining simply to decoration and general neatness
and cleanness could not so engage public sympathy and interest
as to call forth the necessary funds. This lethargic and unfortunate state of public opinion was not much altered at the time
of Sir Hugh's accession to the civic chair ; men still clung to
their purses, and loudly deplored the unfortunate condition of
St Andrews. He had, therefore, to encounter nearly equal disadvantages with those who had previously contemplated the reformation of the city ; and no predecessor in the provostship had
rendered the way smooth before him, or removed difficulties and
impediments from his path. Unaided, save by his efficient and
actively co-operating brother magistrates, he undertook to achieve
that which had baffled so many, and his efforts were successful
and his triumph complete.

When Sir Hugh's projected improvements were first spoken
of, they were highly applauded, and gentlemen of fortune and
independence in the town and neighbourhood only lamented
that the Town-Council had so scanty funds in their possession
to carry the improvements into execution. It was now Sir
Hugh's object to show that there was no cause for such lamen-
tation and discouragement, and that gentlemen simply required
to put their hands in their pockets, and bring forth the necessary
help. This doctrine, so startling and novel, of course was very
difficult at first to digest ; but at length, influenced by the
Provost's liberal example, influential and wealthy citizens began
to disburse, and, touched with a kindred feeling of enthusiasm,
eagerly endeavoured to prevail on their neighbours and friends
to go and do likewise. The taper once ignited, spread into a
brilliant torch, which gradually expanded into such a powerful
and resplendent blaze, that every dark and dreary alley was
destined to receive speedy and thorough illumination, and every
disagreeable excrescence and disfigurement to be entirely uprooted

and destroyed by its burning lustre. Every individual citizen became personally interested in the general work of improvement —every merchant contributed according to his means, every artizan gave his mite, each member of a family his contribution. Nor were the neighbouring gentry and occasional visitors allowed to escape ; all had to table their quota of the general voluntary taxation—all visitors to St Andrews had at least to profess to share in the general enthusiasm. The hearts of the fair population were also won, and the ladies of the city and neighbourhood eagerly sought how they could forward the great work of reform. With one simultaneous movement they began to make use of their fair fingers in the preparation of fancy and embroidered work for a Ladies' Sale, which, being attended by the gay and fashionable from all quarters, produced an immense addition to the funds. Thus, in a remarkably short period of time, a large sum was deposited in the treasury, to be laid out in the improvement of the city, as the Provost's wisdom, skill, and prudence might suggest.

The first great work of public reformation effected in the city, was the laying of a complete line of foot pavement along each side of the south or principal street, from end to end, viz., from the West Port to the *Pends*, or ancient great entrance to the precincts of the Abbey. In the laying of this pavement, the Provost had what seemed to many an insurmountable difficulty to encounter. From the irregular joinings of the houses, and the many uncouth and unseemly outjuts, porches, and projections proceeding from the buildings, a line of pavement in front of the houses had necessarily been interrupted, and the consequent turnings and windings would have rendered the promenade unpleasant, would have destroyed the effect of the repair, and would, in fact, have completely spoiled the broad and spacious appearance of the street. But Sir Hugh's genius at once suggested a remedy for these seeming impediments in the way of reform. By happy and good-humoured appeals to the proprietors and occupants, he obtained leave to remove the unseemly projections, uniformly taking care, after obtaining leave from the parties concerned, to have the work of demolition proceeded

with early on the following morning, completely to guard against
any change of resolution. To remedy the unequal joinings of
the houses, the line of pavement, about four feet in width, was
placed at a considerable distance from them, and appeals were
then made to the occupants of the houses along each side, to
seek their own comfort and convenience by laying down pavement at their individual expense, in front of their respective
houses, to join them with the main line. The suggestion was
necessarily followed, and in the space of another twelve months,
each side of the street presented a continuous line of pavement,
in many places to the breadth of fifteen feet.

Many anecdotes are told about the diplomacy displayed by Sir
Hugh in getting this magificent pavement laid down. When
it was first proposed, the proprietors of houses would not hear of
it all; it would never do; people would walk close to their
windows, and pry into their secrets. Sir Hugh gravely acquiesced in this view, and proposed to lay a 4 ft. 6 in. pavement
at a distance of 12 or 14 feet from the houses. This was quite
a different thing; so the owners agreed, and the Provost had
the viaduct laid through the waste of rough causeway. The
consequences may be easily guessed. The inconvenience and
bad look of the rough road intervening between the narrow strip
of pavement and the windows, actually compelled the proprietors to finish the foot walk at their own expense, and this street
now boasts a fine *trottoir* of an average breadth of 18 feet.

Another triumphant feat of the Provost's was the removal of
an obnoxious court, surrounded with several hideous trees, which
projected 15 feet across the pavement. The tenement was occupied indeed, but the occupant was in arrears. Said the Provost to the owner, " I will guarantee your rent if you give me
a line to get you possession by removing the trees and porch."
The proprietor was charmed at the prospect of getting his rent,
and acquiesced. Sir Hugh handed over the rent, and the owner
went to sleep over his agreement, which he was very likely to
rescind in the morning. But when he looked forth at early
dawn of next day, behold! there was not a vestige left of the
horrible eyesore; trees, porch, and walls had vanished, stick

and stone. A whole chapter of "projection-removing" stories could easily be made from this part of Sir Hugh's history.

Among the other disfigurements of South Street, to which we have already alluded, were the dirty, gloomy-looking aspect of the building of the West Port, a number of heavy and hideous erections for wells along the sides of the street, the absurdly expansive railing round the Town Church, encroaching on the street, and the dismal and heavy appearance of the structure of the University Library. These the Provost put speedily to rights—the West Port was painted, ornamented, and provided with elegantly cut tablets of the arms of the city, &c., the uncouth wells were substituted by a few handsome and convenient erections; the railing was removed in a night, and a handsome new one erected entirely free of the street, and the building of the Library was tastefully ornamented and painted.* The erection of the elegant houses at the corner of Castle Street, and the great and manifest improvement (at, however, enormous expense to Sir Hugh) on the old " Black Bull Inn," now named by him " Victoria Buildings," have added much to the beauty and magnificence of South Street ; and were undertaken by this liberal-minded and public-spirited man, SOLELY with the view of improving the appearance of the street. The substitution of elegant square lamps on the pillar lamp-posts for the old-fashioned round ones, has wonderfully improved the appearance of the street at night, and rendered it one of the best lighted in the country.

South Street was shortly afterwards rendered a safe and quiet

---

* Among the other defects and disadvantages which St Andrews possessed prior to the Colonel's reign, was, particularly, the ruinous and dismal-looking condition of the houses ; those even of the better sort being uncouth from want of cleaning, and comfortless from want of care. Many of the old and inferior houses the Colonel prevailed on the proprietors to remove, and to erect magnificent and comfortable-looking buildings in their stead, while the better houses were externally painted, adorned with columns at the doors, and otherwise improved. So enthusiastic has the Colonel been on this subject, that when the proprietors hesitated to effect the repair, he made purchase of the property himself, and at his own expense decorated the buildings. This was no *unfrequent* act of his.

thoroughfare for carriages, which it had not been from time im-memorial, the wretched *boulders* used in forming the pavement producing inequalities and a general roughness, which caused many accidents, and created an unnecessary noise in the ears of the peaceful citizens. To carry out this improvement, the Provost succeeded in having all the old pavement removed, and ordered the better part of it to be used in repairing the sides; while, by an arrangement with the County Road Trustees, he got the centre on the roll of the Turnpike Roads, and accordingly had it neatly *macadamized.* The improvement is immense, the rattling of carts and carriages being wholly unknown, and such a thing as a horse coming down never heard of. Paved crossings were provided for the use of the citizens, and every care taken to have the whole street kept clear and convenient. The surface of the street was so judiciously arranged, that showers, instead of in-juring, tend to improve the thoroughfare, running as soon as they fall, into the sewers at each side, carrying away the super-fluous sand and mud into the ocean.

A series of improvements on the Harbour and its vicinity also formed part of Colonel Playfair's programme. Among the first of these may be mentioned the removal of an old vessel which had lain in the harbour for many years, and which possessed a rather peculiar history. It had been arrested for debt, and the parties to whom it belonged continued to live in it till it became completely dilapidated, the water running in and out of it as the tide rose and fell. The spars and upper works disappeared bit by bit, till nothing but the hull remained, blocking up the har-bour-way, an eyesore to everybody. The energy of the Provost, however, overcame its dead weight, and it was made to march in the general progress of renovation.

Considerable improvements were made on the approaches to the Harbour; the whole roads, walks, and boundary walls, par-ticularly those on the road leading from the Pends, which had long been in a ruinous state, were put into a state of complete repair. The piers and slips, also, underwent substantial im-provement and renovation; and as the sea had encroached con-siderably on the eastern side, a powerful and substantial barrier was erected, which has successfully resisted all further damage from that quarter, and bears ample testimony to the wisdom of the Provost's plans. The Harbour was widened and deepened.

In connection with the Harbour, an important improvement must now be mentioned,—the erection of a Lantern on the north-west turret of the Cathedral Wall.* Seamen had often experienced great difficulty in making for the harbour in thick weather, and several accidents had consequently occurred in the bay. This lantern, known by the name of the *Turret Light*, is 100 feet above sea level, visible five miles, and is known to mariners as a stationary white light. The lamp was, on the urgent solicitation of the Provost, erected at the expense of the Commissioners of Northern Lights, and is kept burning at the expense of the Town's funds. On the evening on which the light was first exhibited, the 12th February 1849, a grand procession of all the seamen belonging to the city, accompanied by large numbers of the tradesmen, &c., took place by torchlight. Shortly after 7 o'clock, the procession, headed by Neptune with his mighty trident, supported by the British colours, and accompanied by the instrumental band of the city, a full-rigged ship, and a glorious display of flags and streamers, moved from the Kirkhill along North Street, and then along South Street to Sir Hugh's residence. Here the procession drew up in a body, and Neptune, having stepped forward from the ranks, rang the door bell, and brought forth His Honour from his dwelling amid the joyous shouts of the assemblage. Immediately thereafter, the mighty monarch of the deep, through his adopted son, presented

* We may here take occasion to remark, that all the improvements in the City during the Provostship of Sir H. L. Playfair have been carried out with the utmost regard to the preservation or renovation of the ancient architectural remains. It is evident, from the natural position of the Turret, and from other circumstances, that it had been constructed as a light tower, to afford guidance to mariners navigating the dangerous Bay. There is a turret of a similar nature at Arbroath Abbey. The Cathedral Turret has thus, after the lapse of centuries, been restored to its original purpose. Before Sir Hugh's accession to the civic chair, matters in this respect, even in recent times, were very differently conducted in the City: the most venerable fragments of antiquity being sacrificed to serve the most trifling purposes of temporary expediency.

to the Provost the following address, congratulating him on the noble exertions he had made to promote the safety and welfare of the numerous family of the ocean monarch engaged in ploughing the grand though tempestuous expanse of his royal domains :—

To the Most Noble the Provost of our ancient and sea-girt City of St Andrews,

THESE, GREETING.

NOBLE SIR,—At a late hour, and in scenes remote from hence, I did learn by a sea-nymph, late on yesternight, that many of my sons were this evening to pay a just tribute of thanks to you for your unwearied toil in doing good to all ; but more especially in having, after great care and labour, obtained the erection of a lamp on an old watch tower of your city, as another polar star to guide my family while ploughing my own dominions. I deemed it due to you, of whom I had heard so much under the Line, to hasten as by electricity and rail, to head those of my hardy sons who were to do themselves honour while paying this mark of respect to one who has ever been ready to promote every useful and social improvement. I do therefore most fervently thank you for what you have now done for the benefit of my sons, and shall ever keep it in due remembrance ; and wishing you a long and happy life, with no short grog and banyan days, I am graciously yours,

NEPTUNE.

Signed and Sealed at our Coral Cave, }
   this 12th day of February 1849. }

The following address, signed by fifty-eight shipowners and shipmasters connected with the river Tay, was also presented to Sir Hugh :—

To H. L. Playfair, Esq., Provost of the City of St Andrews.

FERRY-PORT-ON-CRAIG, February 1849.

SIR,—We, shipowners and shipmasters, engaged in the foreign and coasting trade in connection with the river Tay, beg to express to you our most cordial and hearty thanks for your persevering and successful efforts in gaining the aid of the Commissioners of Northern Lights to the erection of a lamp, to be lighted on the 12th current, on the north wall of the Cathedral grounds of the ancient city of St Andrews, of which you are the worthy and energetic Chief Magistrate, and which we understand is to be lighted in future at the expense of the incorporation over which you preside.

We can assure you that the benefits you have, by your kind and gratuitous exertions, bestowed on the shipping interest by the erection of this lamp, is by us, and will be by all mariners frequenting this portion of the east coast of Scotland, highly and sincerely appreciated.

Wishing you health, happiness, and length of days to carry out many useful and salutary improvements, in the face of all groundless opposition, we are, Sir, your obliged and faithful servants.

(Signed by fifty-eight Shipowners, &c.)

The Provost then, in a very affecting manner, read the following reply :—

GENTLEMEN,—By the interest you have taken in the birth-day of my little son, you have evinced feelings which do you much honour ; for the Turret Light is to be a great benefit to your fellow-creatures navigating the Bay of St Andrews, and your sympathy for them shows that your hearts are in the right place.

Your gratitude to the Commissioners of Northern Lights has been nobly exhibited. By such demonstrations you prove yourselves worthy of receiving greater favours.

Long may you live to enjoy the advantages of the light which is this evening kindled. When overtaken by violent winds and a raging sea, and guided by this friendly star to your happy homes, you may thus address the Lamp of the Turret,—

Well placed art thou on the hoary tower,
A light to the bold and the free ;
Shine on, happy type of celestial love,
As our guide in the stormy sea.

After a variety of cheering for the promoters of the Turret Light, the procession left the Provost's residence and proceeded to Gregory's Green, where it broke up and formed into various companies, who spent the remainder of the evening in rejoicing.

The Muse was also propitious on the occasion, several poetical pieces having been written in honour of the event. As specimens of these effusions, we subjoin a verse from one of them.

THE NEW LICHT.

TUNE—Woo'd an' Married an' a'.

You've heard o' our Provost, " The Major,"
The lord o' St Leonard's wide ha' ;
There's nane but Field Marshal " the Duke"
Kenn'd better or farther awa'.
But, oh ! had you seen our auld city,
An' heard how his praises were rung,
When first the New Licht o'er the waters
Its bricht an' its cheery beams flung
Licht an' lantern an' a',
Lantern an' licht an' a' ;

An' shouldna our Provost be sung
Wi' his licht an' lantern an' a'.

. . . . . .

In connection with the Turret Light, and as showing the
spirit of opposition that Sir Hugh frequently met with, we give
the following extract from the *Fifeshire Journal* of that date,
and also the whole of the poem referred to. "While on the
subject of public improvements, the late erection of a lantern on
the top of one of the turrets of the Abbey Wall is an improvement for which seafaring men will thank the Provost; yet this
work, called for by humanity, has, we regret to say, very much
hurt the fine feelings of some of the enemies of improvement,
who reprobate it sentimentally as 'a desecration of the beautiful ruins.' Of course, the probable saving of a ship and her
crew and cargo would be very dearly bought at the expense of
a wound inflicted on the delicate taste of these gentlemen. On
this subject we feel great pleasure in directing the attention of
our readers to the finely imaginative poem in this day's paper—
a beautiful fiction fraught with a most instructive moral."

THE TALE OF THE TURRET;
A CANDLEMAS CAROL.

In an Abbey Tower sat a Bat one night,
  Too heavy at heart to fly;
And he told his grief to a churchyard Mole,
  That had crawled from his tunnel nigh:
" They have soldered a lamp to my nest, alas!
And they'll light it up with the Company's gas!"

" Wise friend," said the Mole, "your case is droll;
  But mine is a worse mishap:
While they patch at your Turret, they poke and prowl,
  Till they make each turf a trap:
And we engineers, undermining the ruin,
Find our snouts chopped off ere we know what we're doing.'

So the Mole and the Bat, and the Bat and the Mole,
  Squeaked out a song in chorus;
And they praised, in their rhymes, the quiet old times,
  Before there were Provosts to bore us;
And the burden was this,—" Let Earth and Sea
Be dark for the sake of such as we."

But the Spirit that haunts the Prior's tower
   Lay listening all the while :
He had suffered so many alarms of late,
   That trifles provoked his bile.
" We Brownies," he sighed, " might be happy souls,
If it were not for Provosts, and Bats, and Moles !

" And yet, of the plagues of my aged life,
   There are some that are worse than others :
I can't sleep aright, any summer night,
   For the Bats fly-flapping their brothers ;
And, whene'er I awaken I hear with dismay
How the Mouldiwarp scoops my foundations away.

" Now, Provosts (I'd pay to all sinners their due),
   Give a little less reason for grumbling ;
For though I don't relish their mendings much,
   Being mended is better than tumbling.
And the lantern, too !"—Here, as sweet as cream,
He fell fast asleep, and he dreamed a dream.

He dreamt that he sailed, in a freighted fleet,
   Up through the perilous Bay ;
And the night grew dark, and the east wind rushed
   From the clouds of Norroway ;
And over the decks flew the boding foam,
And the mariners groaned when they thought of home !

Lo ! there shot away, from the Turret gray
   That stands on the rocky height,
O'er the lurid spray of the midnight bay,
   A stream of the purest light :
And the sailor was surely a bit of a fool
That didn't like, then, to see rusty Saint Rule !

Then the Harbour, so glorious, was with ships quite uproarious :
   They filled it from Bridge down to Pier ;
Though how they could ever get in or get out
   Was perhaps not sufficiently clear :
And the Harbour-master was proud—Oh, look !
His purse has burst with the dues he took !

But the money-bag's breaking occasioned the waking
   Of the Spirit, who looked rather blue ;
And he scratched, in a puzzle, his reverend muzzle ;
   " Ah ! this is too good to be true ;
Yet blessed be Life, and the Powers that save !
I welcome thee, Lamp of the Northern Wave !"

The old lighthouse, at the end of the pier, was removed, and a pillar and lamp erected on its site, showing a light to seaward of a light red colour, visible four miles, and changed to green when there is occasion to warn vessels of danger in approaching the harbour.

A number of other improvements, of a minor character, were also effected in this neighbourhood. Gregory's Green was completely renovated, the accumulations of rubbish removed, and the road repaired. Lamps were erected, and the barrier at the Dennis Work made safe. The Burial Ground had been long neglected, but the Provost, by strong and urgent solicitation to the Commissioners of Woods and Forests, procured a grant, and had two additional pieces of ground added to it, spacious walks laid out, the surface dressed, and the tombstones arranged, while the whole was surrounded with an elegant wall, with handsome gateways. These alterations were at first bitterly opposed by some of the citizens, but are now universally approved of.* He has repeatedly applied to the Commissioners to have the graves levelled, the tombstones placed in regular order, and the cemetery greatly enlarged, and there is reason to hope that this excellent improvement may yet be carried out. Sir Hugh likewise effected great things with regard to the Burial Lairs, by obtaining the consent of Government to appropriate the ground he purchased to the poorer classes, free from payment; and he it is whom we have also to thank for having the grounds all open to the public.

It had long been the custom for the female part of the fisher

* Another of the innumerable instances of opposition to Sir Hugh. In the course of the formation of the walks, a number of the citizens complained to the Commissioners of Woods and Forests that an unjust infringement was made on their rights, and that the Provost's doings here were painful to their feelings, to have regular promenades formed in the place where their departed relatives were interred. From the strong language of the complainers, the Commissioners were induced to suspend their operations, though, fortunately, previous to this representation, Sir Hugh had the principal promenades formed, —so that, on the whole, the improvement seems to be complete. It certainly was to be regretted that this movement on the part of the citizens did occur, as unquestionably the introduction of spacious promenades in the burying-place of the dead, was calculated to produce an agreeable impression on the great body of the living. This is indeed one of Sir Hugh's great works.

population to carry mussels and other bait from the Eden in baskets on their backs—a custom productive of much indecency. The Colonel, with consent of the Council, ordered carts to be provided at the expense of the Town, in order to the abolition of this indelicate practice; and though at first "the ladies" strongly resisted, they soon found it their duty to submit to the opinion of their acknowledged benefactor. The mussels are now conveyed to the town in carts, as they are required, at a price per cart agreed on to be paid by the fishermen, according to the quality. The state of this part of the town was also, by Sir Hugh's energy, greatly ameliorated, and a gradual course of improvement entered on, introducing many comforts and privileges to which the fishers were previously utter strangers.

Their wretched and demoralised condition had long been complained of by the cultivated and respectable portion of the citizens, and many fruitless attempts had been made, for a long period, to rescue them from their state of filth, misery, and degradation. Every attempt towards their reformation had always been met with the basest ingratitude; every kind word with abuse and disrespect; and every act of charity and benevolence was spurned at and contemned. The respectable citizens then, for the greater part, looked on with pity mingled with dread; and by all was this uncivilized and unfortunate class looked on as too polluted to approach. The Colonel fearlessly undertook the task of reformation, boldly entered the haunts of misery and dissipation, accosted the inmates in the tone of authority and command, and called on them, as rational beings, to arouse from their slumber of wretched degradation.* He was completely successful. Whether by the dread of his authority, or force of his persuasion, the wretched abodes of filth were cleaned out; the inmates, to a considerable extent, were prevailed on to cherish temperance, or even total

* We have been informed that, on Sir Hugh's first inspection of the fishers' houses, or rather hovels, he found that instead of removing their rubbish to the street, that it might be removed by the scavenger, they had been in the habit of retaining it in their attics, or somewhere within their walls, and that the accumulated layers of horrible nuisance he discovered were sufficient to have raised a virulent pestilence.

abstinence from intoxicating liquors, and instead of spending their money in the dram-shop, and indulging in the practice of blasphemy and Billingsgate, to clothe themselves and their families, to fear God, and to reverence authority. A school has been erected for their children, under the superintendence of the Rev. Dr Cook. A reading room for the general use of the body was fitted up; and following Sir Hugh's example, the citizens stored it with many useful and appropriate new publications, as well as works of standard merit. We are, however, sorry to learn that this is now discontinued. An arrangement was also made to enable them to hear a sermon preached by an authorised missionary at least once a-week, and tracts and other small religious publications distributed among the individual families.

For the greater comfort and convenience of the fishers, the Provost proposed, a few years ago, to erect for their accommodation a large and convenient building on the East Bents, near the Harbour, to which he intended to attach the imposing name of "Victoria Terrace." However, after the ground for a foundation had, at considerable expense, been prepared, difficulties occurred in the prosecution of the scheme, owing to which it has been abandoned in the mean time.

But while thus vigorously devoting himself to the external decoration of the city, and to the promotion of the general comfort of the citizens, Provost Playfair has likewise displayed a warm interest in the moral and religious regeneration, not of the fisher population merely, but of all classes of the inhabitants.

Encouraged by Sir Hugh, the mechanics, some years since, commenced the formation of a public Library and Reading Room, in which, by the payment of a mere trifle, the works of the most popular authors, and approved and widely circulated journals and newspapers, may be read and studied.

The Mussel Scalps in the Eden, the property of the Corporation, had been allowed to run to waste, like every thing else; but Sir Hugh speedily, though not without opposition, had them so managed, that instead of bringing the small sum of £25 per annum to the Town's funds, the handsome revenue of from £300 to £400 a-year is now derived from this source—this year (1860) the sum realized is £421. For his services in this matter, the Provost was presented with a large mussel shell! set in silver. Had Sir Hugh's system not been pursued, the Town would have been about £3000 in debt more than at present.*

The Madras College was also the scene of some of Sir Hugh's labours. To him it owes much of its renown as a scholastic institution; to him the pupils owe much of their comfort in the school, and much of their amusement out of doors; and to him is due that interest which is taken in the School by all classes, both in the town and neighbourhood and at a distance. The educational arrangements have been modernised and improved from time to time as occasion offered; while every thing relative to comfort and convenience, alike of masters and pupils, has been strictly attended to. A portrait of Dr Bell was placed in the Trustees' Room, and a bust in stone, by a native artist, was placed on a pedestal under the ruin in the front of the College, the ruin itself being strengthened and thoroughly repaired, and the whole enclosed from the street by a handsome iron railing. A very fine organ was erected in the great Hall, to assist in the musical education of the pupils; in this room a large stage was also erected, to hold 120 children, for the purpose of more effectual teaching; and the playground was made perfect by the erection of a complete set of gymnastic apparatus. The heating, ventilation, &c., of the various apartments were also attended to, the buildings annually kept in thorough repair, and the whole finances, &c., &c., of the College placed on a satisfactory basis. To particularise and detail all the various improvements he effected here would occupy a small volume of itself; it must therefore suffice to say, that by Sir Hugh's energy and well-planned alterations, the Madras College is now second to no institution of the kind in the country.

The zeal of the Provost is further exemplified in the complete renovation of the Infant School. This institution was situated in a very unsuitable locality, in a large ill-ventilated apartment at the back of the Town Church, since converted into the City

* The net profit since 1813 amounts to £2713, 13s.

Hall. Seeing the propriety of its removal, Sir Hugh obtained a grant from Government, a sum was also given from the Bell Fund, and aided by the active co-operation of the other city authorities, the present handsome and convenient structure was erected at a cost of £800, from a design furnished gratuitously by the late Mr Nixon. The building was afterwards surrounded with a piazza, for protection to the children in wet weather, and the play-ground gravelled and neatly laid out with shrubbery. Any one looking at this beautiful spot now, and remembering what it was before, a collection of dilapidated cow-houses and dung heaps, will heartily coincide with the Provost in his brief but emphatic declaration, " This is my first child!"

The old building at the back of the Town Church was afterwards converted into a spacious Hall, which has been found very convenient for public meetings, auction sales, and the like. Shortly after its completion, about two hundred of the citizens and others assembled in the new hall, at a public supper, on the 27th October 1845, when Provost Playfair's health was drunk with all the honours. In the earlier and palmier days of the burgh, the chief magistrate seems to have been designated by the imposing title of Lord Provost, a distinction which has fallen into desuetude, and which the present chief magistrate is not ambitious to revive. The following correspondence recently took place on this subject between Sir Hugh and a gentleman in Edinburgh :—

EDINBURGH, Sept. 17, 18—.

MY LORD PROVOST,—I beg you will excuse the liberty I take in addressing you on the present subject.

Having a dispute with a gentleman as to whether the Chief Magistrate of St Andrews is entitled to the appellation of *Lord* Provost, I will take it as a great favour if you will let me know.

I have the honour to be your Lordship's most obedient Servant,

(Signed) J. G——.

The Honourable the
Lord Provost of St Andrews.

ST ANDREWS, Sept. 17, 18—.

SIR,—I have the honour to receive your letter of this date.

The Chief Magistrate of St Andrews is addressed as *Provost* only.

I have no doubt that at an early period (when Edinburgh, Glasgow, and

Aberdeen were villages), the Chief Magistrate of St Andrews was designated as you describe, but when it became common he left it off.

I have the honour to be, Sir, your most obedient Servant,

H. L. PLAYFAIR, Provost

To J. G——, Esq.

Though not officially connected with the University in any way, yet Sir Hugh's influence made itself felt here too, and many improvements and alterations were made on the buildings at his instance. The new part of the United College had been standing unfinished for a long time, on account of part of the grant having been diverted to another purpose. The Members of the University had made repeated complaints to the Royal Commissioners and to the Lords of the Treasury, in regard to the inconvenience to which they were subjected by the building being unfinished, but all in vain, or without any favourable result; till, solely through the active intervention of Sir Hugh, who made a special journey to London on the subject, a new grant of £6000 was agreed to by Government and sanctioned by Parliament for its completion. This new grant, carefully and economically expended, under Sir Hugh's superintendence, was found sufficient to defray the cost of erecting the remaining north wing, in the manner designed on the original plans, while containing much more interior accommodation. An additional sum, however, being required for completing other projected improvements in connection with the College, the further grant of £2600, entirely through the continued exertions of Sir Hugh, was obtained from the Treasury in 1847. This last grant was sufficient to complete the entire renovation of the College. After long and earnest application from the Provost, the whole buildings were placed under the charge of the Crown, thus providing for their maintenance in time to come. In the Library he also effected many improvements; the building was tastefully ornamented and painted. The Professors' Room was entirely refurnished, painted, papered, and decorated; the passages and staircase repaired and painted, and stained glass door provided, &c. This was only finished after an immense amount of trouble and annoyance to Sir Hugh. Into St Mary's College, also, he carried the same spirit of improvement, and the whole buildings were put into a complete and thorough state of repair; the area was cleared out, the long walk laid out and gravelled, and the trees trimmed. The Principal's house was modernised, the hideous porch removed, the house ornamented outside, and the proper entrance to the premises adopted; the coats of arms were also cleaned, recut, and replaced, with many other improvements and renovations.

> " But time would fail, ere half the tale
>   I could declare to thee,
> Of how he fought the Home Office,
>   And banged the Treasurie ;
> And all for the sake of the Colleges
>   And the Universitie.
> Though whether he ever got thanks for the same,
>   Is quite unknown to me ;
> Except being told to write with his name
>   The letters LL.D."

The steeple of the College Church was repaired, and a fine new clock with an illuminated dial provided by the Crown, but never lighted, (it can be for no other reason than to save the expense of the gas burners) ; a new parapet was built round the top, the tower itself pointed and repaired, and the spire provided with a new vane, higher by five feet. The College Church had been surrounded with a hideous old wall, by which much of the beauty of this fine Gothic edifice was hidden ;* this the Provost had removed, and the proportions of the building brought fairly into view. For more than a century the chapel has been used as the parish church of St Leonards. In 1846, at the suggestion, and also at the *expense* of Provost Playfair, it underwent very extensive repair.—The cumbrous shutters on the outside of the windows were removed ; the old pews were entirely taken away,

* Respecting this very ugly obstruction, it may not be improper to remark that, in former times, street projections were viewed by the civic authorities as ornamental. On 3rd July 1782, the Town Council, as appears from their records, granted authority to Dr John Hunter "to erect a paling and wall in line with the wall in front of the College Church, as it would be an ornament to this locality."

and elegant new ones substituted; a tastefully executed new pulpit was erected; the walls were oil painted, and decorated with elegant gas lustres; and the very dismal-looking lobby was converted into a spacious vestry. A neatly enclosed pew at the side of the pulpit was fitted up for a choir of singers, to assist in promoting the psalmody of the congregation, &c., &c. These improvements and repairs, mentioned above, were all executed at the urgent solicitation of Sir Hugh, who expended upon them an immense amount of time and trouble.

Within the church, on the north wall, and at the end of the cross passage, there has been inserted a very handsome stone and marble cenotaph, in memory of Sir Hugh's eldest son (William), who fell at the battle of Sobraon, in India, in 1846; it was erected by his brother officers, to whom he was endeared by his amiable disposition and sterling character. Sir Hugh's second son (Arthur) was also killed in action, and only about two years after his brother, at that bloody and memorable battle the storming of Mooltan, in 1848. On hearing of his death, the Town Council sent an address to the Provost, deeply sympathizing with him at the very afflicting tidings.

We must state, ere we proceed further, that to furnish any thing approaching to a full and accurate catalogue of the repairs, decorations, and improvements which are directly traceable to the efforts of Provost Playfair, would be a task of *no ordinary magnitude*, and would require an acquaintance with every nook and corner of the city which few, save the indefatigable Provost himself, can possess. The best idea of their nature, importance, and extent that can be conveyed to the public is, that Sir Hugh has exclusively devoted his time and attention, and the whole energies of his soul, from his accession to the civic chair till the present time, in planning, superintending, and executing them. We must content our readers by simply noticing some of the principal and most conspicuous of a thousand and one improvements that have taken place in the city up to the present time.

Many improvements were made on the roads and walks on the outskirts of the city. In particular, the Scores Walk, along the north of the town, had long been unheeded, and permitted to lie besmeared with filth and interrupted by hillocks. The Colonel ordered all obstacles to be removed, threw down unnecessary hillocks and impediments, levelled and cleared the whole extent of the walk, tastefully decorated part with grass and part with gravel, and formed a promenade almost unequalled in any town in the empire.*

The walk known by the name of the Lead Braes, extending from the Plash Mill to the foot of Abbey Street, deservedly a favourite from its many beauties, was also thoroughly repaired, and commodious seats erected here and there.

We now come to speak of several street improvements which Sir Hugh carried out most successfully to completion. The entire laying of the principal streets with pavement, and general causewaying, was a gigantic undertaking, assisted as it was by but a small sum from the public funds. But Colonel Playfair had his old Indian experience to back his energy of purpose. Here is a specimen of his bulletins and appeals to the public :—

TO THE INHABITANTS OF ST ANDREWS.

LADIES AND GENTLEMEN,

You have done much in contributing to the Improvement of your City, but something more remains to be effected.—The Market Street should be supplied with FOOT PAVEMENT on both sides, from Union Street to Bell Street. It is for you to determine whether this shall ever be accomplished. The City of St Andrews, through the Town Council, have this day subscribed £50 towards this object, in their anxiety to increase the comfort of the people, and the beauty of the city. If other Public Bodies will imitate this example, and contribute according to their ability, this great purpose may be accomplished. The Ladies, by a SALE OF WORK, might do much. The Householders in Market Street will, of course, lend their ut-

* Curiously enough, while Sir Hugh was engaged in levelling the many unseemly hillocks in the vicinity of the Martyrs' Monument, and gently sloping the banks from the Monument to the Links, a number of philippics appeared against him in the provincial papers, accusing him of destroying and disfiguring the *natural* beauties of St Andrews. What Sir Hugh must have endured from the foolish and ignorant, in carrying out even the most evident and laudable work of reformation, very few, if any, have the slightest conception.

most aid, and it is expected that other Inhabitants will assist them, as they did when called on to subscribe for the South Street Pavement.

The amount required is £252. If this sum is subscribed the work will be commenced—if not subscribed the amount guaranteed by the City will be withdrawn, and the Market Street will remain in its present deplorable condition, much to the discomfort, may we venture to say, much also to the discredit of the Inhabitants of our venerable City and its Vicinity.

St Andrews, 14th March 1846.

Having thus "*paved the way*," operations in Market Street were forthwith begun, and by means of subscriptions and otherwise, it was completely repaved from end to end ; the huge old boulders, across which the inhabitants used to estimate their powers of agility by hopping from stone to stone, were all removed, and a neat causeway substituted ; a four-feet line of foot pavement was also laid down on both sides of the street. At the western end, the street was considerably widened and otherwise repaired and improved.

North Street was acted on in like manner. A broad line of causeway was laid along the centre of this street for its whole length ; excellent water channels were put down on both sides, to carry off the surface drainage, while the space between them and the centre causeway was neatly gravelled. Foot pavement. of the same width as in the other streets, was also carried from end to end in front of the houses ; a number of projections were also shaved off or taken down altogether, so that on the whole the appearance of this street is now very little inferior to South Street. These improvements were finished in 1854, and the successful completion of them loses no merit by the fact that the Episcopal Congregation, as well as some of the principal proprietors in the street, did not contribute a shilling towards the expense.

The northern part of Bell Street, extending from North Street to Market Street, had been completed for some years, but immense difficulty was experienced in prevailing on proprietors and other parties to agree to allow the street to be carried on, as originally intended, to South Street ; and, indeed, for some years the proposal was considered as abandoned. In 1845 Sir Hugh put his shoulder to the wheel; and though it was the expectation of many who were unacquainted with his powers of persuasion, that he would be unable, without a special Act of Parliament, to overcome the obstinacy, and allay the scruples, of so many parties decidedly opposed, the achievement was speedy and complete. When the street was completed and the thoroughfare opened, it was at once considered a most surprising improvement, as it afforded direct communication between the Madras College and the northern and western parts of the city, and was found to be highly useful by the inhabitants. The whole of the site was purchased by Sir Hugh for £2000, and for some considerable time the surface of the street was his private property, but we hope he has long ere this been fully reimbursed. The benefit and convenience of this opening is *incalculable*, and it has done more for the prosperity of the city than it is in our power to describe. It unites the three streets by a central communication, improves the value of property in each, and connects the Infant School with Madras College. We regard this achievement as among the GREATEST in the City.

Soon after South Bell Street was fairly opened to the public, there remained for some time a footpath obstacle, in the shape of a projection of one of the old houses. This, however, was in good time removed, in spite of the obduracy of the proprietor, and it deserves mention on account of the characteristic manner in which it was accomplished by Sir Hugh. He caused pavement to be laid as far as the obstruction, and as he humourously remarked, " By opening the street, he was enabled to direct the stream of public opinion against it until it fell."

.   .   .   .

St Andrews ! weel I mind the day,
   Each rugged, lichtless street
Seemed just the picture o' decay—
His destined and undoubted prey ;
The streets grass-grown, the mire-dubs lay
Wi' od'rous relics i' the way,
   To smoor the passing feet.

But soon there dawned a brighter day
  Upon the ancient city,
Auld nuisances were swept away,
Improvement marked the civic sway.
Whase the good deed, ye Muses say?
Hugh Playfair's name shall grace my lay,
  And ornament this ditty.

There is an old Town Hall planted, as was the custom of old, in the middle of the street near the Market Place, interrupting the thoroughfare more than any projection, of such plain architecture as to be no object of attraction in the town, and in *many* respects has long been considered totally inadequate for the wants of the community.

On this ill-planned edifice the Colonel cast the eyes of his destructiveness soon after his accession to the civic chair, and would have had it swept away *at once,* if he had only had funds to erect another in what he thought a more suitable locality. To procure these he at once determined; and following the motto of his life, " Do it, and 'tis done," he lost no time in setting about the matter. The task he had proposed to himself was a difficult one. But the effort was worth making, and unceasing were the varied ways in which he sought to engage attention, and enlist in the matter sympathy and support. In desperate anxiety to have his heart's desire fulfilled, he issued the following handbill in 1843, which will serve as a specimen of similar proclamations :—

NOTICE UNIVERSAL.

It is hereby intimated to all those who have or who may have any funds at their disposal, and who are hesitating to what purpose they will apply them during life or at their demise, that the ancient city of St Andrews is a field where a bequest might be made for a purpose which would perpetuate the name of the donor to future ages—namely, to furnish the means, either by deed or gift, for removing the present Town Hall from the centre of the street, where it is a great obstruction and deformity, and to build another which should contain a market-place, assembly rooms, and other conveniences, thus securing to the donor the gratitude and blessings of generations to come. Any person feeling inclined to promote this great public work, will receive every information on the subject, on application to Major Playfair, the Provost of the city.

This undertaking was in abeyance for fourteen years after this effort to set it agoing ; and it is testimony to the unflagging purpose of its originator, that in 1858 his intention was carried into effect, and the foundation stone of a new Town Hall laid in South Street, opposite the Town Church. This building contains a Council Room, houses for Constable and Town Officer, two Lock-ups; with a Great Hall, 75 feet by 35, and 24 feet in height, with dressing rooms and other accommodation for public assemblies. The arms of Scotland are over the main entrance, those of the city on the corner tower, and those of Sir Hugh and Dr Bell over the great window on the north.

Sir Hugh gave the handsome subscription of £100 to this great undertaking, besides getting up two different Ladies' Sales, which realised the large sum of about £500. He was also the means of procuring many additional subscriptions to the fund from his country and city friends.

Meanwhile, the old hall had been renovated, by being painted, papered, and otherwise repaired and made serviceable for a time. A commodious covered market-place was also erected at the east end.

Sir Hugh first essayed in his private capacity as a citizen and keen golfer, the regeneration of the beautiful Links. A company of golfers had existed since 1754, under the title of the Royal and Ancient Golf Club of St Andrews, but little system was observed in promoting either the amusement of members or the facilities for playing the game. There was no kind of club-house, no brilliant assemblies on medal days, no trim-kept Links ; in fact, if the town was slovenly, equally so was the Golfing-Links. The Colonel, in 1833, instituted a primitive kind of Club-house in connection with a body of Archers (mentioned in all the histories of the town), with a subscription of 5s. per annum ; and this modest beginning was the nucleus of the strong association, under whose auspices the development of St Andrews is so distinctly and rapidly advancing. Afterwards, the Club grew stronger and he had a small building at the end of Golf Place fitted up for its accommodation, containing convenient dressing-rooms, a billiard-room, reading-room, &c., the whole put under the charge of a steward, and opened by the Provost 26th January 1835. This establishment, called the Union Club, has remained under Sir Hugh's charge ever since, assisted by two Directors annually chosen.

The prosperity of the Association increasing through the Provost's indefatigability, and much comfort having been derived from the unpretentious building it occupied, it was considered judicious to erect a commodious and permanent Club-house. Accordingly the present building was completed in 1854, and Sir Hugh handed over to it, from the accumulated savings he had amassed by his masterly financiering and judiciousness, during the time he had been Manager and Secretary of the Association, the large sum of £850. From this it is easy to perceive what invaluable services he had rendered the Association since he became its originator and manager. He also subscribed to the building himself in the most handsome manner. A magnificent full-length portrait of the Provost, as founder of the Club, painted by Mr Wilson of Glasgow, hangs in the large room, and a miniature likeness, presented by Mr Rodger, is also hung in the reading-room.

To gratify citizens, strangers, and more particularly the ladies, who might wish to witness the game without being present on the Links, comfortable seats were erected on the top of the Witch Hill, and other eminences around, from which the course of the golfers might be viewed. The sea had long made encroachments at high tide on the eastern portion of the Links, often inundating an important part of the golfing ground, and carrying away portions of the surface. Sir Hugh, at considerable expense, erected an embankment to resist the fury of the waves, which was filled up inside with earth and sown with grass, completely preventing all such encroachments in future, and gaining a considerable extent of surface for the operations of golf.

On New Year's Day 1855, Provost Playfair had the satisfaction of issuing the following *ukase*, which is significant of the success attending his past labours, blended with a characteristic desire still further to advance the town's prosperity :—

ST ANDREWS, Jan. 1, 1855.

FELLOW CITIZENS,—In consequence of the cleanliness of the streets, and the taste displayed in ornamenting the houses, the fame of St Andrews has spread abroad. This well-deserved celebrity is rapidly extending. Strangers from every quarter are induced to reside amongst us. Workmen of taste and ability are ready still further to decorate your houses. If they are employed, your dwellings will have a more attractive appearance, and you will have the satisfaction of contributing to uphold the glory and prosperity of your beloved city.

H. L. PLAYFAIR, Provost.

It would be difficult, almost impossible, as has been remarked before, to tell of all the remarkable changes for the better which are directly traceable to the efforts of Sir Hugh, but from among them we may select the following :—

TOWN CHURCH.—In the course of Provost Playfair's improvements, this church was surrounded in front with a magnificent new iron railing and parapet, the old barricade being pulled down, and ground acquired to the street ; the enclosed ground being at the same time neatly laid out, and planted with shrubs and evergreens. Broad walks, from the gates in the railing to the doors of the church, were also laid with pavement. But to curtail as much as we can—The north side was enclosed with posts, the well at the corner removed to the back of the church, water channels constructed, and the whole remodelled. But his great reformations here were not merely confined to the exterior of the building ; he effected many improvements in the interior of the building as well. The Vestry, formerly a small uncomfortable room, was, by his highly meritorious exertions, enlarged and fitted up for the accommodation of the Presbytery, who hold their regular meetings there. The room was regularly fitted up with pews for the audience, and very comfortable seats for the members of court, who enter by a separate door. A magnificent pulpit, adorned with rich crimson velvet, and surmounted with a cross, was erected for the moderator. The fine old city bell, also, was rendered secure, and made to ring after a silence of 25 years ! At a meeting of Presbytery held shortly after all these operations had been completed, Provost Playfair had awarded him the thanks of the members of Presbytery for his activity and exertions.

CEMETERY.—We previously omitted to state under this heading, the great things the Colonel here effected with regard to the " Burial Lairs," by obtaining the consent of Government to appropriate, free from payment, to the working classes, the ground which he succeeded in having purchased ; and Provost Playfair it is to whom thanks are due for having all the grounds open to the public.

THE CASTLE.—Numerous renovations and resuscitations have been made in the square, and many interesting remains brought to antiquarian light. Like the other ruins in and around the city, the Castle has recently been extensively repaired, and entirely freed from the encumbering mass of rubbish, so that a pretty general idea is now afforded of what it was when entire. The more recent excavations have brought to view part of the moat and the piers of the drawbridge, in front of the building; and in the centre of the area the well was discovered, cleared out, and a parapet and rail was erected round it from stones found in the well, to guard against accidents.

DENNIS WORK.—This was a breakwater of rough stones, below the Cathedral Bank, commenced in 1517 by Prior Hay, but never finished. The sea had made considerable encroachments here, by undermining and washing away portions of the cliff, whereby the safety of the Cathedral wall was endangered. By Sir Hugh's exertions, a substantial wall or breakwater was begun, and after considerable difficulty and interruption from storms, brought to a triumphant completion, and the cliff effectually saved from further encroachment. A lamp was also erected to prevent accidents at these precipices in dark nights; another was also erected at the entrance to the Fishers' School.

THE PENDS.—At the urgent request of Sir Hugh, the tottering walls were pulled down and rebuilt; some curious coins were discovered in one, and are now to be seen in the Museum. A fine road and footpath were made to the Harbour, and a water-trough provided for horses and cattle.

ABBEY WALL.—This, together with the ruins of the Cathedral and others adjoining, received considerable reparation, and had many of the encumbrances removed, &c., and thus rendered more worthy the inspection of the curious.

WATER.—A large additional supply was obtained by the assessment being raised from one penny to fourpence in the pound, after much excitement and opposition; and though the supply is still too limited, much benefit has resulted from the improvement. The pipes were numbered and understood for the first time by the Committee.

STREETS.—" Eyesores," projections, porches, and obstructions of every kind removed. (If the consent of the proprietors was obtained in the evening, the porches or projections were in general completely removed before the appearance of the morning sun; his reason for this was, we suppose, to guard against any change of resolution.)

CASTLE STREET.—In order to improve the appearance of this street, Sir Hugh himself purchased the wretched-looking and hideous old house known as "John Dibb's," pulled it all down, and in its place erected the present building, containing upwards of 16 rooms, for the poorer classes. The Parochial Board refused to purchase it, and bought two old houses instead, not nearly so well adapted for their requirements. This improvement, however trivial to appearance, was the means of costing the Provost a great deal of money (and, we doubt not, much bother), but the exact sum we are unable to state.

UNION STREET (formerly called Foul Waste)—was considerably improved at the north and south ends. In ARGYLE, the whole channels were lifted and relaid. CHURCH STREET was lifted and reconstructed. COLLEGE STREET was widened and paved, and an elegant new house erected at the south-east corner. CITY ROAD was widened, railing brought forward, wall built, and permanent depot for road metal secured. BUTTS WYND, also, was widened and improved.

SLAUGHTER HOUSES.—After ten years' endeavours, a new and commodious *abbatoir* was built to the south of the city, and all slaughtering within the burgh prohibited.

BATHS.—A pool was here excavated in the rock, for bathing in any state of the tide, and safe and convenient foot paths, &c., constructed for the accommodation of the ladies. At the WITCH LAKE the roads were also improved, the Steps recut, &c., for the convenience of bathers.

LADY BUCHAN'S CAVE.—This famous place, which was long unapproachable from the rocks having been washed away by the tide, the Provost had rendered of safe and easy access to visitors; and he must have been either a very timorous or indifferent visitor who could not then seat himself in the rocky cell of St Regulus.

MINERAL WELL.—This chalybeate spring, situated at the East Rocks, was cleared from the debris which had fallen from the cliff above, a basin constructed to receive the water, stones placed so as to protect it from the sea, and the spot rendered of much easier access.

MARTYRS' MONUMENT.—This neat structure also dates its origin from Sir Hugh, at whose instance it was erected and neatly railed in.

CLEANSING DEPARTMENT.—A complete and most efficient system of scavengering has been organised, which is inferior to no town in the country.

CITY REVENUE.—Last, though by no means least, through the Provost's measures the City expenditure was reduced below the revenue.

In closing this list of improvements, we must not forget to mention an occasion on which the renovating hand of Sir Hugh experienced a complete check. Many were the engagements he encountered before he was enabled to carry out, with success, his plans for the ornament and improvement of the city. The opposition, too, was often of the most bitter and violent kind; and sometimes proceeded from parties to whose public spirit he might rather have looked for co-operation and support—or, to say the very least, for *favourable consideration;* and yet, there were found those, who, profiting largely by his labour, would yield him none of these, not even the common courtesy of neighbours, when their own interests were, though ever so slightly, involved. Surely if any man's conduct be deserving of a favourable interpretation, we must grant it to him who " lives laborious days" for others— to him who, " spurning inglorious ease," is ever toiling for the common weal. In attempting to repair a walk on the south side of the city, so as to complete the circuit of the town, Sir Hugh was arrested in his endeavours to beautify St. Andrews.

A little stream comes down from the uplands of Strathkinness, and, taking upon itself the name of the Kinness Burn, tumbles merrily and very prettily along a sheltered ravine hard by the southern limit of St. Andrews city, till its tiny waters fall into the harbour. Along this rivulet there is a charming walk. It meanders along the bank from the very harbour, up to, and beyond, the busy mill-wheel at Law Park. Before the Major's time, no attention had been paid to the keeping of this footpath in repair ; and, from the soft nature of the ground, it afforded far from comfortable footing, being very slippery in bad weather, very rugged always, and liable to injury from *spates* in the burn, as well as from the ebbing and flowing of the tide.

The Major, who had ever an eye to comfort as well as the picturesque, and had bettered other indifferent paths before, turned his attention in 1843-44 towards the civilisation of that neglected but tempting walk by the margin of the Kinness Burn. You may easily fancy that no time was lost. The Major's cohort was soon at work. Out came mattock, spade, and levelling tube ; and, by voluntary subscription, the Provost speedily succeeded in forming a trim and delightful walk from the Plash Mill to the steps of the

5

Burn leading to Abbey Street, with the undisputed consent of adjoining proprietors.

In 1848, a difficulty arose in carrying the walk further east, as it had to pass by certain ground belonging to St. Mary's College. The works were impeded until evidence was produced that the inhabitants had been in the habit, from time immemorial, of using the banks of the Kinness Burn, in proceeding from Largo Road Bridge to the Shore Bridge.

Twenty-eight old men declared that they had done so from their youth upwards. These depositions were sent to the College Masters, but no notice was taken of them.

In the progress of repairing the walks in 1849, the Provost continued improving the said footpath, which was much resorted to by the inhabitants on the south side of the town, and for that purpose employed a man named Benjamin Wallace, to effect the trifling repairs requisite for completing the circuit of the city ;* when (can it be credited?) the fury of the law was hurled at him with all the VIOLENCE and SECRESY that his most inveterate and revengeful enemies could devise.

Let us now see the Major at this crisis ; it is worth our while. 'Tis a pet scheme of his, the walk by the dripping, trickling Kinness. He is proud of the good he will accomplish, when all is done. But even this favourite thought is dismissed from his brain on the calm Sabbath evening when we are supposed to be looking in upon him. He is engaged with other and holier themes. It is the Communion Sunday—the calmest season of the civil year. The grey city is hushed in that still repose, emblematical of the holy season. The reverend fathers of St. Mary's College are doubtless reading their breves, and meditating on the solemn sacrifice which had that day been commemorated, oblivious of the bustle and jangling interests of this sublunary scene.

* The repairs referred to were these :—The footpath was merely smoothed, and made more passable,—a plank or two was placed over a ditch which ran across a part of the footpath ; and at the east end of the walk, near the Shore-Bridge, to prevent the necessity of jumping over the wall, a slap was made in it where a slap used to be, and a turnstyle was placed therein to prevent the ingress of cattle, by all which any person could conveniently walk along the banks of the Kinness Burn without in any way or manner interfering with any arable land ; indeed, the very reverse.

Sir Hugh, we said, is sitting reflectively in his arm-chair. A summons comes to the door—again, and again, the startling call sounds through the stillness of the sacramental Sabbath-eve. There are sounds—and the tramp of a knave-in-office, and presently a myrmidon of the law makes his appearance in the Major's presence, and serves the astonished Lord Provost—*O! tempora o mores!* with an interdict from the Sheriff.

An interdict? but against what? You may well ask, for the Provost himself had no conception; with shame and humiliation we write it, this interdict was taken out at the instance of the Professors of St. Mary's Theological College, against the Major, to prevent and stop for ever, the improvement of the Kinness Burn promenade! Yes! they had no sooner heard that his reformations had extended to a paltry footpath alongside their property (which would in no earthly manner have injured it, or diminished it one farthing per annum in its rental), than with collegiate power, all reckless of daily words of kindness or even neighbourly good feeling or generosity, they summarily proceeded to interdict these reforms by legal means, and without giving him any opportunity of explanation either personally or through their agents, or even warning him that they were going to take legal steps against him.* Had they only afforded him extrajudicial notice, matters would doubtless have been arranged to mutual satisfaction.

History recordeth not what the Major did when he read that astounding document; but probably he did what posterity will certainly do when it peruses this authentic account—rubbed his eyes.

There it was, however, black and white. It would have been atrocious enough if the venerable fathers had gone down to St. Leonard's in person (as many of them had done for purposes of hospitality in times past), and said:—

"Major, we admire you hugely. You are reviving our importance. You are bringing students to our colleges. You are, in fact, letting people know, even those at a distance of ten miles,

---

* In so far as the Kirk-session was concerned, not a whisper of opposition was heard—that body having always been among the Provost's most anxious supporters in his every attempt at moral, religious, and social improvement.

that there *is* a college for divinity here. May your shadow never be less! But on no account are you to make this walk! We can't have it—you are trespassing on the very hem of our priestly garment—namely, on the very edge of an exceedingly valuable field. We regret it exceedingly, but if you go on, it will be our painful duty, in the cause of religious freedom, to pull you up short with an interdict."

But the aforesaid fathers did nothing half so courteous, and the end of it was that the interdict was actually taken out, served, and sustained as above related!!! As a specimen of the spirit in which the action was conducted, we give the following passage from the mandate subscribed by the four ministers of St. Mary's College on December 8, 1849 :—

"We hereby certify that we authorised Messrs. Grace and Yoole to raise said action forthwith, without communication on the subject with Major Playfair."

Not choosing, at his own individual expense and risk, to battle this right of way with the pursuers, he, at dawn on Monday morning, ordered everything to be made just as it was formerly, at his own expense, and, by nine o'clock the same morning, the footpath was rendered as impassable as it was before, and matters were all restored to their former disagreeable condition. Thence commenced the legal proceedings against the Provost.

Some zealous friends volunteered to defend the action before the Sheriff at their own cost. The pursuers put in a minute, acknowledging that matters had been restored, but insisting for their expenses; and therewith they produced a mandate by them to their agents, Messrs. Grace and Yoole,* certifying that they had authorised them to raise the action, and to follow forth the same to a conclusion; and it most unfortunately terminated in the patriotic Provost having all the expenses incurred by the other party to pay from his own pocket. How exceedingly and deeply it must have pained the public spirited man to be dragged into court at the instance of these worthy pursuers in such a manner.

* A curious anomaly appears in this action, viz., the Town-clerks, Messrs Grace and Yoole, were the agents for St. Mary's College, being the factors, against the Provost, yclept a residenter only!

The Sheriff, in pronouncing his interlocutor, made the following reservation in the cause of generous sentiment and gentlemanly feeling, and evidently regretted tho decision which, by law, he was compelled to give :—

" The course so promptly pursued by the respondent, in restoring matters to the former condition, affords a very satisfactory proof that an extrajudicial application on the part of the petitioners would have rendered the present proceedings in court unnecessary,—

" Considering that in these operations the respondent could have no other motive but to benefit the public in the manner set forth in his pleadings, the Sheriff cannot help thinking that the petitioners might have had the COURTESY to have remonstrated privately against the operations complained of. Since, however, they insist on the *summum jus*, the Sheriff feels that he has no alternative but to find the respondent liable in the expenses of the application."

As the case created considerable excitement at the time, we subjoin a letter from the *Fife Herald* to shew the feeling that was entertained upon the subject by the public :—

DOINGS IN ST. ANDREWS

To the Editor of the Fife Herald.

SIR,—On a recent visit to my *alma mater* in Fife, I found myself almost a stranger, so many of the inhabitants whom I had formerly known had left the city, or were dead : but the great magician happily still survives, who has transformed the city and university from what they were twelve years ago to what they are now, and is too well known to your readers to make further allusion to him necessary at present.

Having been educated at the United College, I naturally felt some interest in the city, and, by accident, my attention was called to a document which, though very ancient, has only within these few years come to light and been printed, namely, a charter by Robert, Bishop of St Andrews in the twelfth century. It runs thus—" Robert, by the grace of God, the humble minister of St. Andrews, to all the faithful, as well future as present, *salutim*. Be it known to you, that, by the help of God, and the permission of David our King, we have appointed a burgh at St. Andrews, in Scotland; and in this burgh, we have made Maynard, or Fleming, provost, with the consent and confirmation of the King. And to the said Maynard, and his heirs in the said burgh, we grant, on account of his services to us and ours, three tofts, &c, &c. And because he is among the first of those who began to build and restore the said burgh, we earnestly entreat our successors, that for the love of God, of St.

Andrews, and of us, they will love and cherish him and his heirs; and let no one do him or his any injury, on pain of excommunication," &c., &c.

This remarkable allusion to the first provost of St. Andrews naturally recalled to my mind the existing provost-magician already alluded to; and I doubt much, nay, I feel all but certain, that there is no provost in Scotland that can trace back so remote an official pedigree as the chief magistrate of this burgh; or one, therefore, who, in consequence of the foregoing charter, is so well entitled to all the honours of his rank and station. And more especially is he entitled to such honours from those ecclesiastics in this city who claim to be the successors of the venerable Bishop Robert. Yet you may guess my surprise, Mr. Editor, when I was informed (with what truth your St. Andrews readers will know) that the very reverend gentlemen who can with propriety be called the Bishop's successors (inasmuch as they have succeeded, by law, to his *status*, and to a considerable part of his emoluments), so far from "loving and cherishing" the present Provost, who is unquestionably the successor of Provost Maynard, that they have been lately doing everything in their power, not only to annoy him personally, but to thwart him in his laudable endeavours to improve the city!

He got into a dispute, it seems, with the ecclesiastics above mentioned, who are the professors of the Divinity College, in an attempt he made to improve an old footpath, extending from the Largo Bridge to the Shore Bridge, where there had been a right of way from time immemorial, because, forsooth, it passed along the edge of a field belonging to their college! The use of this pathway, when improved, it was admitted by all I heard speak on the subject, would have been of great benefit to the inhabitants, and no injury whatever to the college field. And yet these rev. 'gentlemen, without even previously warning the Provost that they were going to take legal steps against him, served him with an interdict which they procured from the Sheriff! and to make bad worse, they served this interdict upon him near to midnight on the eve of the Sunday set apart for the half-yearly dispensation of the communion!! The following were the instructions issued by the successors of Bishop Robert to their law-agents, in regard to the successor of Provost Maynard—"We hereby certify, that we authorised Messrs. Grace and Yoole to raise said action, forthwith, without communication on the subject with Major Playfair."

Just after my attention had been directed to the above hostile proceeding on the part of the said ecclesiastics towards their Provost, who might have expected better treatment at their hands, I chanced to take up a newspaper in which I found, with unmingled satisfaction, the following delivery from the St. Andrews Presbytery, which had assembled to address the Queen on the all absorbing question of the Papal Aggression—"As ministers of the God of peace, we follow peace with all men, and cultivate that charity which suffereth long and is kind." This is precisely the language and behaviour which every consistent Christian would wish to see emanate from divines, and I was the more refreshed by it, from my mind having been previously somewhat soured by reflecting on the opposite conduct I have been adverting to. If any of the professors of the Divinity College were present at the Presbytery meeting, they must have felt painfully the contrast between their own conduct, and the heavenly language of their brethren here quoted. But in case they were not present, I cannot better end this epistle, than by calling their attention to it through the medium of your widely circulating paper, in the hope that they will see it, and lay it to heart, and in all time coming, act in accordance with its truly Christian spirit.—I am, sir, very faithfully yours,   VIATOR.

DUNDEE, 1st January 1850.

P.S.—Since writing this letter, I have been informed, that not only all the professors of the Divinity College were present at the Presbytery meeting, but that one of their number actually drew up and read the address containing the language above quoted. But this must be a mistake; I can never believe it.

Another writer, who knew well about the matter, has given another and more brief, but, it must be confessed, somewhat bitter account of it. As it affords further explanation and insight into this most remarkable circumstance, and may be perused with interest by those who are curious about the manifestations of human meanness, we make no apology for presenting it. After sketching and commenting upon the Provost's works of reformation in the city and environs, the writer goes on to say—

"So far, the success of Sir Hugh was unchecked and almost unchequered except by the whispers and criticism of those uncommonly prudent and excellent people who shake their empty heads at, and find fault with every new thing, particularly if it look like an improvement. But in one instance, this extremely natural propensity to resist all kinds of reformation took an active shape, and was in a measure effectual. The walks around the town had all been repaired and rendered passable for other bipeds than ducks, under the Provost's directions, with the exception of one leading along the banks of the Kinness Burn, which the public had used as a footpath from time immemorial. That path ran along by certain lands belonging to St. Mary's College, and it was not to have been anticipated that the learned professors of this school of divinity would have opposed anything so reasonable as the mending of the public way. But they had consulted a legal person of the name of Yoole, who, after laboriously ransacking his stores of learning in the law, gave them to understand that repairing a public footpath was an inversion of the state of possession and an atrocity to be put a stop to by interdict. Fully satisfied of the soundness of this pundit's views, the professors of divinity thought it right to oblige him with a job which, with the delicate reluctance peculiar to the higher branches of his profession, he obligingly undertook, feeling extremely averse in his heart to stop any public improvement, but still more averse to lose an occasional 3s. 4d. or 6s. 8d. for telling a brother of his craft in Cupar what to do,—he firmly believing himself to have a faculty for giving directions and advices, in all matters of religion, politics, ethics, or law. The result of his application for interdict rather tended to confirm this modest belief in himself, for the interdict was obtained in the sheriff-court of Fife; and although the grounds on which it was granted, have always been a puzzle to lawyers, who are of opinion that a right of way involves a right to keep the path passable, Sir Hugh abandoned this attempt in disgust, being resolved to fight the battles of St. Andrews against every body except professors of divinity, and every where except in petty courts of law."

This, then, is one of those RANCOROUS and UNPARDONABLE cases of opposition which Sir Hugh has experienced in his St. Andrews career, and which must have been indeed grievous to bear; and, although it is the only one that was *litigated*, we believe there have been two others which could be mentioned, which were the means of preventing improvements far more magnificent and important.

They were, perhaps, more trifling in the result, but originated in feeling and dispositions certainly not less paltry and despicable; indeed, too much of both to be worthy of having ink wasted on them.

Such is but an imperfect and short sketch of the Colonel's exertions and services in reforming and renovating the city. He has been a patriot in a true significance of that vague term. He has marked out for himself a barely possible sphere of usefulness, and within that circle he has confined himself. The results are widely and gratefully known, so as to make the Provost and his doings proverbial.

His fellow-townsmen have not been unmindful of his high deserts.

In 1844 he was invited by all the respectable citizens to a public dinner in the Town Hall, to evince the appreciation of his services, and estimation of his worth; but this public testimony he very respectfully and modestly declined.

In 1846 he was requested to sit for his portrait, which having agreed to do, a very beautiful painting, and striking likeness of the patriotic Provost issued from the studio of Sir J. Watson Gordon, of Edinburgh. The portrait was presented to the Colonel at a public breakfast; to which he was invited by the numerous subscribers and others, who, to testify their respect for a public benefactor, assembled in the city on this auspicious occasion. We subjoin an account of it as abridged from the report in the public journals:—

BREAKFAST AND PRESENTATION OF PORTRAIT TO
PROVOST PLAYFAIR.

On the 10th April 1847, a breakfast was given in the Town Hall of St. Andrews, on occasion of the portrait of Provost Playfair, painted by public subscription, being for the first time exhibited to the public. At nine o'clock upwards of *a hundred and sixty* ladies and gentlemen sat down to breakfast. Mr. A. K. Lindesay, of Balmungo, occupied the chair, with Provost Playfair on his right, supported by Sir David Baird and Sir D. Brewster; and Mr. Lindesay of Straiton and Mr. Blair of Cookstone on his left.

Grace was said by the Very Rev. Principal Haldane.

After breakfast the Chairman rose, and addressing Provost Playfair, said —The Committees that have had charge of the arrangements about to be brought to a termination this morning have done me the honour to choose me to occupy this chair, and however great may be my apprehension that I shall be unable to do justice to their choice, yet the duty that I have to perform is to me a most pleasing one. The picture about to be displayed has, as you are aware, been painted at the desire of your fellow-citizens; it is intended to remain as a lasting testimonial of their grateful feelings for the very important public services you have rendered to the community since you were called upon to preside over the municipal affairs of our ancient city. We meet, sir, in every quarter of our town with improvements for which we are sensible we are indebted mainly to your perseverance, skill, and taste. The more we reflect, the more does it excite surprise that so much has been done in so short a time; indeed, the nature and extent of the additions to the comfort of ourselves and of our families, as well as to the beauty of our venerable city, are such as could scarcely be credited, except by us who have seen them grow up, as it were, under our own eyes. But those who see and admire these results may be told that they bespeak not half the labour that you have been zealous enough to bestow. You had not to select and approve from plans already well matured, to glance now and then at the execution of the works, and to order payment out of an overflowing exchequer; no, sir—you had to originate the movement —to enlist public sympathy—to reconcile various interests—to engage in numberless correspondences and conferences—to give close and constant personal inspection—to undertake many journeys—in fact, it is but a few days since you returned from a successful visit to the great metropolis, where the support of the Imperial Government itself was engaged to aid in completing works of great beauty and of permanent usefulness; in short, sir, you had to find "ways and means"—no easy task—but the objects of your aim have been pursued with an energy and a constancy which have been rewarded in the end by eminent success. I am restrained by your presence from doing more than thus hinting at what you have done, and at what you merit from our hands. In too many instances where communities have sought to manifest gratitude to public benefactors, years, nay centuries, have been allowed to elapse after the grave had closed over the mortal remains of those on whose name and memory the honours were conferred. We, sir, have great reason to congratulate ourselves that we have you here among us in full vigour, and, we hope, with a long career before you of private happiness and of public usefulness. May you long continue to preside over the civic councils of St. Andrews—to sit at the feet of that portrait—to follow your own example, for none other can I hold up more worthy.

At the conclusion of Mr. Lindesay's address the cloth was removed from the portrait amidst the applause of the company. The painting, by Mr. Watson Gordon, is very beautiful, and the portrait a very striking likeness.

Provost Playfair in reply said,—Gentlemen, the sentiments so well expressed by my respected friend Dr. Lindesay, in the name of the committee and sub-scribers who have taken an interest in the proceedings of this day, evince so much kindly feeling towards myself that I know not in what terms to acknow-ledge my obligations to them. The whole of your proceedings in this matter have been carried out in a manner the most delicate and complimentary, entailing on me a debt of gratitude which I never can repay. I need not attempt to express how highly I estimate this flattering testimonial of your approval of my past services. The honour you have conferred upon me on this occasion has placed me in a position much more prominent than I deserve to hold—a distinguished position to which few men attain in their native city, be their talents, their merits, or their deeds, ever so great. That picture is placed in the Town Hall, with the consent of the Town Council, as a mark of their approbation of the manner in which I have discharged the duties of the situation to which I was by them elected. It is now some forty years since my attach-ment to this city commenced. Throughout my career in life that attachment has never abated. To return to St. Andrews in the evening of my days for years continued to be the most ardent desire of my heart. When hope dawned on the prospect of realising my fond wishes, I purchased my present abode before I could return to inhabit it, in order to rivet one link of the chain which was to bind me to it during life. Providence continued to bless me, and I returned to my native city to be the humble instrument of carrying out the views of my colleagues in the various works which their wisdom suggested —the expense of which the unprecedented liberality of the people so muni-ficently defrayed. The situation which I have held has afforded me every facility in meeting your wishes on all occasions, and the kind and efficient support of the inhabitants for years past has rendered this duty a delight-ful occupation. Many respected gentlemen residing amongst us in this city have aided me by their counsel in recommending measures which had a tendency to improve the physical and moral condition of the people. In carrying out such suggestions I have ever felt the greatest interest. In justice to the municipal representatives with whom I have acted for some years past, I feel it an imperative and pleasing duty to declare that I have never found them influenced by any other consideration than the welfare of this city, with which all our interests are identified, and that their cordial support has always been cheerfully given to every measure involving the well-being of the town, the advancement and permanent prosperity of which appeared to them an object of paramount importance; and I may, with perfect truth and sincerity, include, as being actuated by the same motives, the whole of the intelligent constituency of St. Andrews. When my children in after times look upon that picture, they will regard it with veneration and respect, and say, "This is the return which a grateful people made to our father for the affection he through life evinced for his native city, and its inhabitants." And may I indulge the hope that my successors, when looking there, may be stimulated to devote a portion of their time and attention to the objects which, for some years, I have pursued with an earnest desire to render the inhabitants comfortable and happy. Any attempt of mine to express my feelings on this occasion would be fruitless. I am aware that what I have said contains little of what I ought to say to you for the distinguished honour you have been pleased to bestow on me. This mark of your regard will inspire me with fresh ardour in your service, and give strength to my feeble endeavours better to deserve your favour during the few years I may yet be spared to enjoy the happiness of dwelling amongst you. May the blessing of our heavenly Father rest and remain on you all, and may our city increase in holiness, and become a pattern for others to imitate! May the inhabitants enjoy every comfort this world can afford, living in peace and unanimity one with another; and may plenty be found to supply the wants of the poor and needy! Once more, accept the expression of my fervent gratitude for this splendid testimonial of your esteem.

The Rev. Mr. Cook of St. Leonards said he had been called on to address the company as one of the committee by whom the portrait had been placed in this hall, there to remain for generations. After the interesting ceremony which they had witnessed, and the interesting addresses which they had heard from their Chairman and from their distinguished guest, anything that might follow must be tame. Besides this, he did not believe that they were here to-day to listen to long speeches. They might be more inclined to do that had it been after dinner: but after breakfast every one was accustomed to hie away to his business—the doctor to his patients, the lawyer to his chambers, and the Provost to his daily walks. As, however, the Chairman's word was law here, he would endeavour to narrate the steps which had been taken with a view of testifying the sense entertained by the public of the services rendered to the community by Provost Playfair, and which had ended in procuring the beautiful picture now before them, and which they would all admit did the highest credit to the artist by whom it was painted. It was as like the Provost as it could be, though it represented him sitting, and they were not much accustomed to see him in that quiescent attitude. They usually saw him moving about with great energy, but painting could not represent him in that way. This was, however, a truly admirable likeness, and would bear comparison with any he had yet seen of Provost Playfair. They had seen one in the London *Illustrated News*, which formed a hideous contrast to this; and it was really a fearful thing to think that the people of Great Britain should all have the idea that the portrait in the *Illustrated News* was like the man whom they delighted to honour. He thought then it was a pity that the Provost had gone up to London. On account of the college and the interests of the city, he rejoiced that the Provost had gone to London, and that he had been successful in procuring a large sum of money to be expended in this city. But the evil was not without remedy. Let an engraving be made from this painting, and a copy of it sent to the London *Illustrated News*, with a request that something like it be inserted in its pages, as the only way in which reparation could be made for the injury which had been done to the fine figure of their Provost. To proceed, however, to the history of this testimonial: Its earliest origin might date from the time that the Provost first stepped from the floor of this hall into the civic chair. As to the portrait, the arrangements for procuring it were commenced when he was absent from St. Andrews in the north; when he returned he found a committee in full operation. The proposal was readily and warmly entered into, and it is truly, in the words engraved on the tablet of the picture, a tribute from the inhabitants of St. Andrews, "in grateful acknowledgment of the benefits conferred upon the city by Major Hugh Lyon Playfair, the present Provost, chiefly through whose patriotic spirit, zeal, and energy, great public improvements have lately been effected." The improvements of the city were aided by various circumstances; but of what avail would these have been without Provost Playfair at the head of affairs? Let him go on in this career, and he could promise him that he need not fear that the inhabitants would desert him. He would now conclude this history. At different times a desire had been manifested on the part of the public that something should be done in honour of Provost Playfair. It was proposed to name a new street after him, and call it Playfair Terrace. Now, with all respect for Messrs. Ireland and Murray, he could not see how they could wish to call a bit of a street after the Provost. It was indeed a very elegant place, but still it was but half a street. There was another terrace that claimed the name. Enter by the West Port—there's Playfair Terrace before you. As you walk along South Street, and admire its magnificence, those who knew it of old could not help being reminded of the distich—

"Had you seen this fine road before it was made,
You'd have held up your hands and blest General Wade."

These and many other improvements around St. Andrews led many of them irresistibly back to the olden times, and they could not help wondering what their forefathers would say if they could return and see St. Andrews as it now was; and he now thought he could see some light as to the reason which had led the Chairman to select him on this occasion to do what others would have done much better. The Chairman was himself connected by a long and honoured line of ancestors with this ancient city; and he (Mr. Cook) had some little connexion also in that way, and was perhaps expected to speak of the olden time. The office which he now held, as minister of St. Leonard's, had been held by Provost Playfair's father, and had been held by his (Mr. Cook's) great-grand uncle and by his great-great-great-grand-uncle; and all he could say was this, that if these men were what he took them to be—men who loved their country and their kind—they would have rejoiced to see the day when St. Andrews would rank so high as it now did in the social scale and in the march of improvement; and their satisfaction would not be lessened by knowing that for these improvements the city was mainly indebted to the son of one of their successors. He would now be permitted to allude to the Provost in his domestic life. There was no man who knew what public life was, who did not know that a public man must submit to many sacrifices of time and of money, and of the very affections; and there was no one who knew Provost Playfair's life who did not know how much of all these he freely placed at the service of the public. His public services involved sacrifices of the comforts of private life, and of the society of those amidst whom, by the blessing of God, he could enjoy the utmost measure of domestic happiness. It gave them great pleasure this day to see so many ladies present; it afforded them an opportunity of publicly expressing their unfeigned regard and attachment to the lady so worthy to be the partner of such a man as their guest. And sure he was, after the way in which they had received this allusion to Mrs. Playfair, that he spoke in the name of every one there, when he expressed their earnest hope that she was pleased with the picture as a likeness of her husband, and as a testimonial of their respect for him ; and that while her wishes might sometimes differ from theirs when they wished to keep Provost Playfair where he is, she would believe that they were not insensible to the obligations under which he was laying them, both to himself and to her; and he was sure that the whole company would join him in wishing health, happiness, and prosperity, to Mrs. Playfair and her family.

The company, after some other speeches and a vote of thanks to the Chairman, then broke up.

The painting now hangs in the Town Hall, decorated with a splendid frame, and will exhibit to grateful posterity the bold, ruddy, and intellectual countenance of one of the *greatest benefactors* of St. Andrews.

In 1849, two magnificent and costly lamps, having the arms of the city beautifully painted on the one, and the arms of Sir Hugh on the other, were placed, at the expense of numerous subscribers in the city, on the columns on each side of his gate, at St. Leonard's, in honour of his graciously accepting the office of Provost for the third time.

The Muse was also propitious on this occasion, several poetical pieces having appeared in the city in honour of the event ; and as a specimen of the effusions we annex one of them :—

THE LAMPS OF HONOUR AT ST. LEONARD'S GATE.

A NEW YEAR COMPLIMENT TO THE PROVOST FOR 1849.

By the Author of " The Major."

A novel Theme the Muse selects at length,
Stretching her pinions doubtful of her strength.
" Rise Honest Muse and sing," in verse elate,
" The Lamps of Honour " at St. Leonard's Gate.
In bright and pleasing colours there we view
The City Arms, and eke the Provost's too;
Type of the pleasant amicable mood
'Twixt Folk leagued only for the Public Good.
Long may these lamps in rival beauty stand.
And coloured splendours dart on ev'ry hand ;
Through many a Lustrum destined to proclaim
St. Andrew's Gratitude—its Provost's Fame.
Hail Ancient City ! once " Of Steeples " named,
But now for Comfort as for Learning famed;

For health and social pleasures thine the meed,
'Mong Britain's Cities northward of the Tweed.
Happy St. Andrews! without row or storm,
To reap each real advantage of Reform!
Long may thy patriots with ready zeal,
Their Cash contribute for the Public Weal.
May feuds political, sectarian strife,
Ne'er vex the tranquil current of their life;
And not a trace of rivalry be seen,
Save friendly contests on the Golfing Green.
Here's to ye, Provost! may it prove your Fate
To wield the Civic Sceptre long and late.
Still may St. Leonard's Lamps of Honour show
Your Popularity with high and low.
And may a lustre brighter far than theirs,
Illume your lengthened path exempt from cares.
Diogenes, in Athens, searched each street
With lamp in hand——an honest man to meet;
St. Andrews hails an honest man in you,
And lights you up not with One Lamp but Two.

In 1850, he was presented with a piece of plate, as a mark of approbation of his management of the mussel bait department, by which, as previously stated, the revenue was increased from £25 to £400 ; this year being even more. The following are extracts relative to the presentation, from the Fifeshire Journal of 1850 :—

Town Council Proceedings.—The Council met on Thursday the 19th December, the Provost in the chair; members present, 23, ... Before proceeding to the ordinary business, Mr. William Smith, on behalf of a committee appointed by the Council in June last, for the purpose of procuring and presenting to the Provost, some token of the Council's gratitude for his services in reference to the mussel scalps, stated to the Council, for the information of those who had become members since the committee was appointed, the reasons which had induced the Council to form the resolution of expressing their gratitude to the Provost for what he had done for the city in improving the mussel scalps. Mr. Smith also produced the committee's report, which stated that they had executed the trust reposed in them, and that they were now ready with the present to be delivered, and they begged that this might be done by their convener. The Council approved of the report and intended present, which was in the appropriate form of a large mussel, mounted in silver, in the form of a snuff-box, with the following inscription :—" Presented by the Town Council of the city of St. Andrews, to Major H. L. Playfair, Provost of the city, as a small mark of their gratitude for his great assiduity in protecting and bringing to perfection the mussel scalps, and thereby greatly increasing their value and importance, 1850." The testimonial was then presented to the Provost by Mr. Smith, accompanied by an appropriate address, and with a renewed expression of the Council's gratitude for the judicious regulations in regard to the supply of mussels now delivered to the fishermen, and the moral reformation resulting from an abandonment of the old habit of the women carrying the mussels to town; as also of the great increase of quantity which the scalps now yield, and consequent increase of the annual income.

The Provost replied as follows:—

"Gentlemen, when on a recent occasion you were pleased to record your approval of my services in the mussel department, you did me more honour than I expected. I felt grateful that my endeavours to increase our revenue were so appreciated. It seldom occurs that an *unanimous* vote of thanks is awarded to any individual for the performance of duties which benefit the city. The pride and pleasure I felt on that occasion. I trust, may stimulate others to merit such a mark of your favour. You had done all you could to inspire me with fresh zeal in continuing the system I had established; but your kindly feeling appears to have no limit; for another more substantial, beautiful, and most appropriate testimonial has now been presented to me, accompanied by such flattering expressions of your approval of my conduct that I really know not how to thank you in adequate terms, nor do I feel that I have deserved such commendation. I receive this handsome gift with the deepest and most heartfelt gratitude, and will ever retain it in my family as a proud testimonial, that the Town Council of St. Andrews knew how to reward the citizens when their conduct met with their approbation." The testimonial was furnished, we understand, by Mr. David Smith, jeweller, St. Andrews.

In 1854, he was nominated by the Hon. the Commission of Woods and Forests, Honorary Custodier of the property of the Crown in St. Andrews.

In 1856, the University conferred on him their highest honour, to wit, the degree of LL.D.

In 1856, the dignity of knighthood was conferred on him by Queen Victoria, as well for the immense good he had achieved in St. Andrews as for the military service he had seen in India.

Seldom has that honour been more worthily deserved; and it was only a fitting mark of recognition on the part of royalty to bestow it on the eccentric and energetic man, who had begged, and bullied, and wheedled away the filth and ruinous neglect which bid fair to entomb St. Andrews as completely as the lava torrents did Herculaneum or Pompeii of old.

But the fame and celebrity of Col. Playfair has not been confined to the immediate scene of his meritorious labours. Since the commencement of his Provostship the greater number of the public prints in the kingdom have eulogised and extolled him, and his name, as a public improver, has extensively become as an household word.

The election of Provost, in St. Andrews as elsewhere throughout Scotland, takes place *triennially*.

The last election for that office having occurred in 1857, it again fell to be filled up on Nov. 9, 1860; and having created more than usual excitement, we give the principal parts of the report of it, which appeared in the papers some days afterwards:—

THE CIVIC CHAIR OF ST. ANDREWS.

(Slightly abridged from the Fifeshire Journal.)

The retirement of Sir Hugh Lyon Playfair from the Provostship had been the subject of remark for some weeks; but our citizens scarcely thought of it seriously until Friday, 2d November, when the following letter was read at the meeting of the Police Commission by the Town Clerk:—

"As the period for which I was elected to hold the office of Provost is about to terminate, and as my name may appear in some of the lists for the next Town Council, I think it right to announce that it is not my intention to accept of the office, should I succeed in obtaining a seat at the Council Board, which would qualify me to hold any of the offices to be filled up when the Council is assembled for the purpose.

" I have neither the health nor strength left which would enable me to perform the various duties required of a member of the Town Council to my own satisfaction; and request that any voter who inserts my name in his list will select another member in my place.

" My warmest and most grateful thanks I now render to all the members in the Magistracy and Council, with whom, for eighteen years, I have so happily and cordially acted, and by whose kind support I have been enabled to carry on various changes—it may be thought by some, improvements—in our city.

" May the blessing of God rest on the inhabitants of this my beloved city, and may it continue to flourish in morality and prosperity.

" Now, my dear Sir, allow me to express my best thanks to you for the kind assistance and valuable advice I have received from you on every occasion for these many years past."

This letter plainly intimated to the public that Sir Hugh was about to withdraw from the civic chair which he had so long honoured, and of which he had made such excellent use. Happily, however, so great an evil has been averted, thanks to the exertions of energetic Councillors, and to the kind assent which Sir Hugh has so feelingly recorded in his ultimate reply to the honour-reflecting address of the members of Council: an assent which, we are sure, will gladden the city at large.

Prepared as we had been for the Provost's resignation, it was no matter of surprise that its public announcement through the newspapers on the 3d of

November, threw the whole city into consternation. A meeting of those members of the Town Council who best knew the Provost's worth, was held on the 5th instant, for the express purpose of devising how best to do him honour, to re-secure his great influence, and to retain his valuable services. With this view the following address was drawn up and signed by the Magistrates and Council-lors of the burgh, and a deputation, consisting of the four Magistrates, was appointed to support its prayer:—

"St. Andrews, 5th Nov. 1860.

"To SIR HUGH LYON PLAYFAIR, Provost of St. Andrews.

"SIR,—We, the undersigned members of Town Council of the city of St. Andrews, beg to express our sincere sympathy with you, on account of the impaired state of your health, which obliges you to retire from the active exertions you have so zealously and so long devoted to the service of this community; and while we can neither expect nor even wish you to continue in the performance of the onerous and fatiguing duties of our Provost, yet, as we cannot cease to identify you with all that promotes the well-being and the improvement of the town, and conscious as we are of the lively interest you yourself will ever retain in our welfare, as long as it may please Divine Providence to prolong your days; and being also desirous to express in some degree the deep sense of obligation we feel, and our warm gratitude to you for the many benefits you have conferred upon us, we now petition you to grant us your permission to return you again as a member of Town Council, in order that we may still retain you as our civic head, *with the distinct understanding* that the active duties of that office shall in future, in so far as you may find necessary, be performed by others, who will be proud to act for you, and under your guidance and direction."

The deputation was courteously received, and hospitably entertained; and after a long and friendly conversation, the Provost stated, with regard to the memorial which had just been put into his hands, that, while he would not object, in the circumstances, to his name being placed on the lists proposed as Councillors, he did not then feel himself in a position to reply to the question of his again occupying the Civic Chair, and therefore decided upon postponing his final answer for twenty-four hours. We believe that his only objection to an immediate favourable response was the too justifiable fear that his future Provostship might be embittered by the recurrence of such personal acrimony as that which had found its way into the previous Council Some such feeling must have prompted, when, in answer to the urgent entreaties of the friends around him, he addressed a naval officer, who chanced to be present, thus:—
"How would you act, Captain, were you again asked to assume the command of your old ship without any assurance of the good character of your crew, and that for so long a voyage as three years?" "Why. Sir Hugh," was the reply, "I would not act at all without a thorough knowledge of my First Officer and perfect confidence in the crew." The deputation was thus encouraged to believe that Sir Hugh's re-acceptance of office might still possibly be obtained; and they accordingly withdrew, resolving to take immediate and effective steps towards securing the return of—what we trust they have obtained—"a most loyal and gallant crew."

On Tuesday evening the results of the poll were communicated to 'the Colonel, which elicited the following decisive answer, upon which we heartily congratulate the citizens :—

"St. Andrews, 6th Nov. 1860.

"GENTLEMEN,—I have the honour to acknowledge the receipt of an Address presented to me on Monday evening, by the Magistrates, and numerously signed by Members of the Town Council, to which, as intimated to the deputation, I should reply in twenty-four hours.

"I feel quite at a loss in what terms to express my feelings on this occasion, or how to thank you, my dear friends, for the high honour you wish to confer upon me, and for the affectionate terms of this flattering document.

"I never can forget or duly appreciate the kindness of the many friends with whom I have so long acted, and from whom, to my sorrow, I was almost, by the force of circumstances, on the point of separation, and thereby of breaking a link of the chain which has so long held us united.

"Your sympathy for the state of my health, so feelingly expressed, and your offer to relieve me from some of the duties which are incumbent on every Town Councillor to perform, deserve my most cordial thanks.

"In meeting your wishes, *on the terms expressed in your address*, I trust in God I may have strength not entirely to disappoint your expectations, whilst I greatly rejoice to be once more a party to labour for the happiness and comfort of our beloved fellow-citizens, and for the prosperity of our city, where, I 'hope, ' brotherly love ' may ever continue to dwell.

(Signed)   "H. L. PLAYFAIR.

"To the Magistrates and Councillors of the
   City of St. Andrews."

Being returned to Council, Sir Hugh, at the first meeting thereof, on the 9th instant, was again installed into the office he has so long and ably filled with advantage to the city and honour to himself.

—————

The following articles, extracted from Chambers's Journal, of January 1844 and October 1847, are understood to be from the pen of an eminent Edinburgh *savant ;* and we the more readily submit them to the reader at the conclusion of our own short and imperfect sketches ; seeing that he will find in them not only an excellent *resumé* of Sir Hugh's doings in St. Andrews up to these periods, but in addition, one or two well wrought pictures of the private residence, the beautiful gardens, and the characteristic daily life and manners of the man, served up, moreover, with so much pleasantry, and in such a style, as cannot fail equally to interest and amuse.

I.—A DAY IN ST. ANDREWS.

"You'll have a tumbling voyage across the Firth to-day," said an acquaintance whom we met on Princes Street, one breezy morning last December, as we hurried along, bag in hand, to the coach-office, whence we were to be conveyed to the sea-side. "Hope not—the wind and tide are together; at all events, can't help it—must go—good-by." "Good-by." The sea, as we came in sight of it on rounding a corner of the curious zig-zag road at Trinity, certainly seemed a little out of humour. There was a white froth on the top of the curling waves, and I half glanced at the possibility of an awkward leaning position over one of the sofas of the steamer. Happily, all such anticipations, proved fanciful. Stepping from the coach on board the steaming craft as it lay close to the pier at Newhaven, we saw there was no danger to be apprehended, and we were soon careering merrily across the Firth of Forth—the shores of Mid-Lothian, with the turret-clad heights of Edinburgh, receding in the distance, and the coast of Fife becoming every instant more and more invitingly open to our landing. The island of Inchkeith, with its grey crags, was passed, and the bay of Kirkcaldy received us into its capacious bosom. In short, we crossed the Firth with little more than an easy breeze, and not a single incident which could be turned to account as an adventure. Nor were we more fortunate by land. A coach which was in waiting, conveyed us without a jar through the peninsula of Fife, and early in the afternoon we found ourselves snugly ensconced in our temporary domicile at St. Andrews.

St. Andrews, as everybody knows, is one of the most ancient towns—we beg its pardon—cities in Scotland. Situated on a flattish promontory overlooking the German Ocean and the Firth of Tay, it appears to have been selected as the seat of a religious establishment by the early missionaries of Christianity who visited this lone and once barbarous part of Britain. Growing apace under the fostering care of Regulus and his successors, the place afterwards became distinguished for its stupendous cathedral—a building in its glory as splendid as the present cathedral of Canterbury—its castle, and its university. Sacked at the Reformation, and with revenues despoiled, its famed ecclesiastical structures sunk into a state of ragged ruins, while its educational edifices merged into an antiquated and forlorn condition, from which they have only been partially restored by some public grants in recent times.* As a seat of instruction, however, the university has always maintained a respectable footing, the place, from its retired character and salubrity of situation, being better adapted for some of the more tranquil branches of study than any of the populous university towns. Latterly, the institutions in the town have been reinforced by the establishment of a large school for elementary education, liberally endowed by the late Dr. Bell, and, at his request, termed the Madras College.

Besides the attractions which may be supposed to arise from its university and schools, St. Andrews offers other inducements as a place of residence. Nowhere in Scotland—and I might take in a much wider range—is to be found such excellent society, or a state of things more harmonious to the tastes and habits of those accustomed to the refinements of life. One is surprised and

---

* Readers curious in the ecclesiastical history and antiquities of this venerable city, may consult a recent work on the subject—"History of St. Andrews, by the Rev. C. J. Lyon" [Episcopal clergyman in the town]. 2 vols. 8vo. Tait: Edinburgh.

charmed to find so pleasant a set of well-bred persons in this part of the world, which is indeed a little world in itself, a thing of which the great, busy, hurry-skurrying world without does not so much as dream. But for this concentration of ladies and gentlemen we must look not only to the educational establishments, but to the out-door play for which the links of St. Andrews are renowned. St. Andrews is the metropolis of golf. Of this game the inhabitants of other cities may *speak*—none but a resident in St. Andrews can discuss it, ex cathedra; all of which the reader already knows, if he has read an account of the game formerly given in these pages. Well, then, golf attracts the lovers of out-door exercise, retired military men, civilians with families, old Indians, and others, from all quarters; while fresh air on a splendid scale, cheapness of living, fine walks, and old ruins full of historical associations, add charms altogether irresistible.

Reader, have you now anything like an idea of the place to which I have come on a flying visit? I am afraid not; for you would require to spend some time in the place to have a complete notion of it—pass an evening with a cluster of its *élite*—see a score of faces gleaming on convivial thoughts intent—hear the laugh of the facetious Professor ———, and be electrified by a toast in Gaelic from Captain ———. The very thought of such a scene makes one feel that this is not such a dismal world after all—that there are nice cheerful nooks in it, if one would only look for them.

Having now, as one may say, taken a bird's-eye view of the subject, we may come a little closer to its main features; and, in short, if you, the reader, have no particular objections, take a look at the town. We have only a forenoon to spare, so let us make the most of it.

Stretching longitudinally along the height overlooking the sea, we find at least three good streets of considerable length, with the ruins of the cathedral closing the vista on the east, and the extensive sandy downs or golf-ground on the west. About the centre of the town, but separated from each other, are the different colleges, and towards the exterior thoroughfares are some new streets of elegant houses. Of course there are numberless cross alleys or *wynds*, generally lined with dwellings of an inferior kind. The whole town is built of sandstone, and is substantial and imposing in its aspect. Till lately, however, little had been done to give it a neat appearance, and it had fallen behind most towns of its size in some few respects; there were here and there, as in several old-fashioned Scotch towns, projections of various kinds upon the lines of street, and even the best thoroughfares were paved only with round stones, anything but suitable to tender feet: smooth trottoirs were unknown. Things might have gone on in this condition for centuries, but for the well-directed zeal of a single individual: I mean Major Playfair, a native of the town, now residing there with his family, and who acceded to the dignity of provost in 1842. This gentleman, possessing an independent fortune, and naturally of an active mind, must be considered as a species of Peter the Great within his burghal jurisdiction. Taking a fancy for improvement where so much was needed, he has already wrought wonders in the brightening up of this venerable city. Any ordinary mortal, three years ago, would have said "Nothing could be done for St. Andrews; her municipal revenue is completely crippled; nobody has any spirit to help her." But on a retrospect, we can see that all such anticipations may prove fallacious when a really energetic man chooses to apply his whole faculties to the object. The greatest doing of the worthy Major is the formation of a smooth slab pavement, of from six to twelve feet broad, on each side of the principal street, along with a double row of gas lamps, as handsome as anything of the kind in the metropolis. Obtaining one hundred pounds, as I understood, from the impoverished burghal funds, the Major had been fortunate in collecting a few more hundreds by subscriptions among the inhabitants and neighbouring gentry, and with this sum he was enabled to carry forward the very beautiful improvement now before us. The effect upon the aspect of the street, which in breadth and straightness was already a fine one, could scarcely be imagined, while its convenience to the inhabitants—supplying a fine promenade, agreeable for the feet, and at all times dry—is no doubt unspeakably great. Great, however, as is this improvement, it is rivalled by sundry other alterations. Everywhere, during last summer, workmen were to be seen engaged in removing old obstructions and eye-sores, propping up venerable ruins, and creating new beauties and conveniences. While other men would plan, ponder, and hesitate, the Major *acts*. Was a railing required in front of Madras college, or a piece of playground to be put in order for its pupils? it was immediately *done*. Was there a street-projection, awkward and incommodious, which had been sighed over and lamented hopelessly, helplessly, for ages? it was one fine morning, before breakfast, *gone*. Was there a too acute angle at the turn of a narrow road, which had been a puzzle to coachmen for a century, and the cause of perhaps two accidents on an average per annum during all that time, but which had in like manner been only bewailed as yet? *now* it was cut off by the Major. Was an unseemly gap to be closed by a neat wall? forthwith the wall was raised. Was there anywhere some particular house so badly placed as to break a straight line, or interrupt a view of some distant object of an interesting kind? the Major would not scruple to lay out a little money, that he might have the pleasure of seeing it removed.

While inspecting some of the wonderful doings of this rare chief-magistrate, we had the good fortune to be introduced to his notice, and conducted by him to different points where alterations had been, or were shortly to be effected. Our first visit was to Madras College, which has been a special object of the provost's solicitude. Conducted from a central courtyard which he has had lately paved, we went through some of the class-rooms of this noble institution, where—hear this, ye Englishmen—a first-rate elementary education may be obtained for a shilling a quarter! In one of the large rooms we found about three hundred children, divided into classes, receiving instruction at this humble charge; and in another apartment a similar number, but of a higher grade, who pay two shillings a quarter. We had the curiosity to examine a class of the humbler pupils, by cross-questioning them on the subject of their lessons, according to what is called the intellectual method, and were much gratified with their expertness. "Wonderful, sir," said the Major, who had kindly taken the chair on the occasion; "what a world this will be in twenty years hence, when these youngsters grow up! They beat us the old set all to nothing." "Quite true, Major; but let us again be stirring." We now proceeded westward towards the principal entrance to the town, where various tokens of improvement met our eye in the form of widening, building, and paving; and turning to the right, we came upon the open links, where we were introduced to the club-house of the Golfers' society. Here are some pleasant accommodations for the gentlemen of the town, including a billiard and reading-room, rooms for depositing golf-playing apparatus, and a species of restaurant, from which refreshments may be obtained at a moderate rate—total annual payment for members ten shillings a year! The doorway, as I observed to the Major in passing out, was rather exposed, and would be improved by a portico. "I know it; you see the foundations of a covered porch are about to be laid." Leaving the club-house, we passed down a street to the eastward, where the Major pointed out some conspicuous improvements; among others an infant-school of handsome architecture, not yet finished, on the pleasure-ground of which his own private gardener was busily at work. Near the school-house the Major proposes various alterations, and some are in progress. As we passed a house which stood somewhat out from the ranks, the Major dryly observed, "Take your last look of it—it will be down by to-morrow morning;" and a cloud of dust which issued from the doorway assured us that he did not speak without warrant. We now proceeded by a narrow pathway overlooking the sea-shore on the north, where several men were engaged in smoothing a most irregular piece of downs, on which a public monument had lately been erected. "Wherever one goes," I said, "he sees people at work." "Certainly; there is not an idle man in the town." Having exhausted this quarter, we went eastward by the united college of St. Leonard's and St. Salvador's, and even here we could see some results of the Major's activity, though not of a direct nature. The doors of the college had been coeval with the buildings—a more shattered, battered, tattered-looking gate did not exist on this side of Somnauth. Within the last two months these doors have shrunk aside into the harmless character of curiosities, and been replaced by doors new and appropriate. The professors had for ages met in a long dreary hall forming a library, and incapable of being heated by an ordinary fire; now, stimulated by example, they have got a smaller room fitted up as a reading-room, where they are perfectly comfortable.

Departing from the college, where some interesting objects of antiquity had detained us a few minutes, we went towards the eastern extremity of the town, near the ruin of the cathedral, where the habitations of the fisher population are situated. Here, the Major informed us, he had great things in contemplation. He proposes that this useful community, whose dwellings are generally old and miserable, shall remove entirely to a spot of ground near the harbour, where he designs to build a terrace of neat and commodious tenements for the different families, on a uniform plan, having in the centre a reading and coffee-room, to which the fishers may resort when on shore, instead of lounging listlessly in the open streets. Means are alone wanting to carry this beneficial improvement into effect; but the work of melioration has already been begun by two improvements, which was entirely the work of the Major. It consists in the establishment of a general conveyance, in the form of a cart, to supply the fishermen with mussel-bait from a part of the coast several miles distant, instead of the old plan, which consisted in each man sending his wife or daughter for a back-load of that material, thus, perhaps, depriving the household of its managing member for the half of every day. A change of this kind, while trifling in the means required for it, is virtually a substitution of civilisation for the grossest barbarism; and its moral are as great as its physical effects. Already, after the lapse of only a few months, a spirit has been raised in this humble community in favour of a more decent and regular course of life. The men are becoming steady and sober, and several female members of families, formerly required for the bait, are getting employment otherwise. The second improvement consists in the establishment of a reading-room for the fishers. In this mind-improving place of resort we found three or four fishermen reading periodical publications, while a row of instructive and entertaining books was ranged on the table before them, and a comfortable fire blazed in the humble grate. For a halfpenny a month, or some such fee, these men can now enjoy a newspaper, cheap periodicals, and books; and for no more than twopence a week, they are supplied with a cup of coffee every morning before going to sea. What a stride in advance is this on the vicious dram-drinking practices to which fishermen are too frequently addicted!

We have now made pretty nearly the round of the town, and as the best of friends must part, so must we bid adieu to the Major. Yet one word ere we say farewell. . . . . . . Here, in little more than a twelvemonth, has one man gone far to accomplish something like the renovation of an ancient and somewhat neglected city. It is true that the patriotic Major has been obliged to open his own purse on several occasions; but this is rather in consequence of the peculiarly reduced state of the burgh funds than from any other cause. The grand requisite seems to us to lie in the qualities of the individual. Let any man of tolerable judgment and taste devote himself entirely for a given time to the effecting of such improvements, and we hold his success to be certain. It can scarcely be necessary to add, that there is classical authority for the inferior share which pecuniary means have in these local phenomena—

> "Who hung with woods yon mountain's sultry brow?
> From the dry rock who bade the waters flow?
> Not to the skies in useless columns tost,
> Or in proud falls magnificently lost;
> But clear and artless, pouring through the plain
> Health to the sick and solace to the swain.
> Whose causeway parts the vale with shady rows?
> Whose seats the weary traveller repose?
> Who taught the heaven-directed spire to rise?
> The *Man of Ross* each lisping babe replies. . . . . .
> Thrice happy man, enabled to pursue
> What all so wish, but want the power to do!
> O say what sums that generous hand supply? . . . . .
> Of debts and taxes, wife and children clear,
> This man possessed five hundred pounds a-year,
> Blush, grandeur, blush! proud courts withdraw your blaze!
> Ye little stars, hide your diminished rays!"

That the provost of a Scottish country town, without the aid of either act of Parliament or tax, should have been able to plan and carry forward renovations so extensive and beneficial, may well excite surprise; and one can very easily imagine, that without a great degree of sagacity, and the most masterly financiering, nothing could have been done. Many are the jokes told of the Major's dexterity in procuring the consent of parties to the excision of street encumbrances, and of his schemes of ways and means. A short time ago, for example, he raised £30 by a public exhibition of pictures lent at his request by families in the town and its vicinity. Nor, from the general tastefulness of his improvements, is there any disposition to ridicule what he has effected, unless perhaps as respects his giving a new nomenclature to some of the roads and alleys, where-by, as with the wand of the enchanter, he has transformed certain wynds into *streets*, thus breaking up, as it may be called, certain old local associations. But even for this he has a ready and tolerably satisfactory answer, which no one actually disputes. Perhaps, however, his greatest act of generalship has been that of stilling down opposition in the municipal body of which he is the head. By the reasonableness of his propositions, his impartial distribution of patronage, and treating the predilections of all men with liberality, being at the same time frank and affable in his demeanour, and ever ready to be consulted by every one, he has introduced the most perfect harmony into his little senate; and it is a fact equally new and gratifying, that no time is ever now consumed in wrangling on general abstractions. This change is not less grateful than it is beneficial to the people generally, and we may be assured that it is no small element in the list of means by which our friend the Major has been able to carry on so many useful reforms. It is a lesson most devoutly to be commended to all the municipal bodies throughout the empire.

II.—AN ANCIENT CITY—ITS IMPROVEMENTS AND IMPROVER.

"*Another Day at St. Andrews*, papa; and this time take us with you, for we long to see what that singular man, Major Playfair, has been doing since you visited the town three years ago." So spoke a young voice representing more persons than one; and being in a mild mood at the moment, I was foolish enough to give an assenting answer. Once in for a promised treat to these youngsters, I always find it the best policy to come to performance as quickly as possible, there being no such thing as rest to be expected in the interval; so the second evening thereafter saw us on our way through Fife by a coach which might be regarded as in interesting and almost affecting circumstances, seeing that on Saturday night it was to be numbered among the things of the past, the railway being announced to open at the beginning of the ensuing week. We felt the tedium of the conveyance, and yet could not, without a sigh, think of even the *last* of a stage-coach. It was evening when we drove into the broad venerable streets of the ancient city. We therefore had no expectation of seeing any of the characteristic features of the place till the dawning of another day. We had, however, scarcely settled ourselves at a late tea, when one of the young people peeping through the window-blind of our parlour, announced the rise of a full-moon of portentous magnitude, and it instantly occurred to us that, the night air being cool and pleasant, we might have a walk before retiring.

Threading some narrow streets and lanes, we soon reached the fine terrace called the Scores, lying between the town and the sea, which here dashes at the bottom of a sandstone cliff of nearly sixty feet in height. I had formerly enjoyed this promenade by daylight, charmed with the view which it afforded of a vast sweep of the scenery of Perth and Forfarshires—for which it seemed only inferior to the Calton Hill of Edinburgh; but I was not prepared for the fine effect of the moonlight in such a situation. While the effulgent luminary rode unbridled through the cloudless vault, the town lay in huge dark masses to the south, tipped only with the aerial silver. In full light, and therefore in strong contrast, rose on the other hand the ruins of the ancient castle, casting a giant shadow backward across the glittering sea. This passed, we speedily came to the ruins of the cathedral and ancient Culdee church, an assemblage of objects at all times fine, but now a perfect romance of beauty. Taking our station on a hillock overhanging the sea, we could see the large churchyard and its monuments fully below our feet, the light being sufficient to enable us to particularise every stone; while from the midst of them all sprung up the isolated gable of the cathedral and St. Regulus' square tower, like irregular twin columns, the moon shining through between them. A side wall of the cathedral, with a row of entire Gothic windows, through which the moonshine poured, had also a fine effect. Glancing from this to the sea, which laboured not more than fifty horizontal feet from the base of the ruins, one could not but attest that a poetry had mingled with the piety of the ancient religious men who chose this situation for a temple. Worthy was it to be the last adopted resting-place of the bones of one who had followed the Nazarene—for in this moonlight the legend of St. Andrew was not to be disbelieved, and it seemed nothing improbable that the whole of the European nations had taken their form and boundaries long after this dark-grey tower was reared! The story, after all, has some plausibility even in a sober daylight consideration, for it is now discovered that the very peculiar architecture of the old church and its tower is *Byzantine*, and a Scottish antiquary lately visiting Patras, whence it is said came the colony of monks who founded it (bringing with them the relics of St. Andrew), found still rife there the very names of the men enumerated in the ancient legend. Henceforth let us not disbelieve a thing merely because it has been related by the indwellers of a monastery.

We prolonged our ramble to the little rough antique harbour, and along under the grand old wall, built by Prior Hepburn to enclose the concerns of this princely religious establishment. Every step of our progress brought out into the moonlight some bit of hoary masonry, rough perhaps with sculpture, or honey-combed by the sea-breezes. Much was coarse, but we felt that nothing was commonplace, scarcely even the matters of present domestic existence which would everywhere intrude. We returned to our inn with a strong sense of the peculiar character of the place, and of the charm which it possesses for impressionable minds.

With the next day awoke an interest in those modern improvements for which the town is now almost as much celebrated as it formerly was for its relics of antiquity. I was eager to renew my acquaintance with that extraordinary Major Playfair who, at the close of 1843, had introduced me to the many remarkable operations which he was then carrying on for the *decorement* of his native city. He was fortunately at home, and with his characteristic promptitude, entered my parlour almost as soon as the waiter who had carried my message. The same hardy strong-set figure, vigorous florid face, and firm hearty voice and blunt manner as before—the same resolute grasp of the hand —the same readiness to do the honours of his domain. "And so, Major, you are still provost, notwithstanding all the good you have done. One would have expected to find your fellow-townsmen tired before this time of hearing your praises." "Why as to that, many of them are heartily sick of my services, and anxious for my promotion. Meanwhile, here am I, still 'my lord,' and at your service." "Well, I wish to see your works now they are comparatively complete: can you be my conductor?" "With all my heart—come along." In two minutes we were in the street.

The South Street of St. Andrews was formerly a handsome and even imposing one, broad, composed of tall and goodly houses, and slightly bending, like the High Street of Oxford, so as to insure a constant change of scenery as one moved along. It was now, however, very much improved from its former self; for, while all those good features remained, a rough causeway, filling it from side to side, had been replaced by an arrangement in which a central line was laid down after the rule of Mr. Macadam, with margins of causeway, while near the houses ran lines of flagstones, forming a double promenade of the most elegant description. This pavement is the Major's great work. It was a thing long wanted for the comfort of the inhabitants; but unless a new pavement for St. Andrews could have been formed, like that of a certain inferior region, of good intentions, there was no chance of its being executed under any former management, seeing that the corporation had no funds to bestow in such a manner. Provost Playfair commenced a subscription amongst the inhabitants, made application to natives and well-wishers of the ancient city, however distant; and by the vigour of his procedure, soon raised the necessary funds. It was no small task; but no one will at all comprehend the case unless he acquires the idea that the Major is a man of genius, of great insight into human character, of wonderful command of argument, and untiring perseverance in working out his ends. He wiled, screwed, pinched, *curried* the money out of men. Very few possessing any means at all could wholly resist him. When enabled to commence operations, he was sleeplessly diligent in engineering and superintending, and thus caused every penny of the money to do the utmost possible work. The lines of foot pavement could not be placed close to the houses, as these were not all in a straight line; it was necessary to lay them at a little distance, and certain irregular gaps were therefore left to be filled with causewaying as of old. This created an unexpected demurrage; but the eloquence of the Major overcame all difficulties, and in the long-run, most of the proprietors of houses filled these spaces with additional pavement at their own expense. The consequence is, that in some places the entire pavement is of princely width; and while individual hardships are forgotten, the community is universally pleased. The indefatigable provost at the same time performed some wonderful exploits, in whisking away certain unseemly projections upon the line of way, using, I believe, all kinds of means for the purpose, even to the expenditure of *not a little* of his own money. In some instances he had these operations effected at an early hour in the morning, so that men wakened, like Aladdin's father-in-law, to see buildings wanting which existed when they went to sleep. A feeling of insecurity took possession of some persons who knew that they stood in the way; and it is told that, in one house which had an elbow pushed into a lane too narrow otherwise, the family kept watch and ward for a night or two while matters were at their highest crisis, lest this modern magician should have all smack smooth before morning. Many, however, caught a happy contagion from his spirit, and commenced volunteer reforms on their property, to the no small help of the general effect.

As we rambled into other streets, I found that similar changes had taken place in nearly every quarter, so that walking in them, from being a penance, had become a pleasure. The means had been procured in various ways—by subscription, by sales of ladies' work, by an exhibition of pictures collected from the *salons* of the neighbouring gentry, everything, I believe, short of downright larceny. At the same time, a thousand small matters of conveniency had been attended to, and a system of careful and thorough cleaning rigidly enforced. Amongst the greatest of the doings of the Major, was the perforation of a dense mass of town with a neat street, serving as a needful communication between one district and another, and which the inhabitants insist upon calling Playfair Terrace. Had not the worthy provost bought up the property for this purpose at his own hazard, it certainly could not have been effected Neatness and propriety were everywhere predominant, excepting only in the fishermen's quarter, and even there, some changes for the better were apparent. The Major, however, had not confined his exertions to his own department. Prompted by his spirit, a well-known millionaire had projected a wholly new *quarter* of the city, to accommodate the many persons in easy circumstances who now flock to St. Andrews, for the sake of its numberless pleasant qualities and circumstances. At the instigation of the Major, the Commissioners of Woods and Forests had laid out the sepulchral precincts of the ruined cathedral in such a manner as to render them an agreeable—at least a solemnly agreeable—promenade, and they were now much resorted to accordingly. He had also taken up the long neglected case of the college of St. Salvator, and succeeded in urging the Government to complete its renovation. This work was now advancing. The rude old hall, which had long been unfit for use, was pulled down, as were several clumps of equally dismal masonry, reared in ages when taste was not, and even comfort hardly had a recognized place in men's affections. In their stead there had been reared a beautiful structure, in the form of a half quadrangle, including not only good class-rooms for the professors, but a large hall of meeting, a private business-room, and a spacious apartment to serve as a museum. An arcade, serving to complete the external decorations of the beautiful old chapel, and a terraced garden, were also in progress. The ancient mother of the Scotch universities must soon, therefore, assume a form worthy of her—a union of ancient and modern edifices truly elegant and graceful. All this is mainly the result of the Major's diligence and force of character, for it does not appear that any other influence connected with the university could have induced the Government to grant the means. The money has been most economically as well as judiciously expended; and the expenditure seems fully justified by the prospects of the institution, which, from various causes, are decidedly brightening.

In the course of our ramble, the young people had seen the chief curiosities usually shown to strangers in St. Andrews. I therefore felt myself at liberty to conclude with a visit to the Major's own residence, which I had heard was amongst the things not the least worthy of attention in the ancient city. I must take some pains to describe it, for it conveys, in my opinion, a most agreeable idea of the domestic establishment of a man living in independent circumstances, and mingling the enjoyments proper to the evening of a well-spent life with the volunteer labours of a public-spirited citizen. Imagine, in a situation retired from the principal street, a long irregular building, partly old, and partly new, having a tall antique structure placed at the opposite side of a courtyard, the whole being the relics of a suppressed college (St. Leonards), but altered to suit the requirements of a private family. Behind the house, towards the south, is a large productive garden, lying beautifully to the sun, and surrounded by ancient turreted walls. Here the patriotic Major and his amiable lady spend their cheerful and hospitable life, surrounded by a blooming troop of children of nearly all ages. The owner's character is everywhere to be traced. In the courtyard, a servant was taking the portrait of a visitor by the kalotype process, of which Major Playfair was an early and successful cultivator. In the lobby, we found some optical instruments, which are occasionally called into use in amusing company. The parlour we found half hung round with kalotype portraits, a perfect gallery of the family's circle of acquaintance, many of whom now live at the distance of half the globe. Amongst these sun-pictures are many presenting groups of ladies, gentlemen, and children, seated in arbours, or under garden trees, or in parlours. These are generally combinations of some portion of the family, with their relations and friends, taken at times when the latter were living at St. Leonard's, or had casually called. The pictures, therefore, serve as memorials of those meetings and associations which often survive so long in memory's waste, but which could by no other available means be recalled in their actual features. Ages hence, if preserved so long, these little frames will depict domestic groups of our era, "in bodily habit as they lived," not a peculiarity of costume wanting or changed. In the same apartment is a series of Indian landscapes, done by various officers in the Major's regiment in Bengal, and presented to him in gratitude for the care he had taken of them, and the instructions he had given to them, when they were young in the service. In his own room, the active character of the man is strongly traced in the numberless philosophical instruments, maps, plans, books, bundles of papers, knick-knackeries of all kinds, which are seen around. One can see it is the retreat of a man who is never one moment idle. It is also visibly the temple of the *practical*, even while something of whim and drollery mingles with most things the Major has to do with.

A door from the dining-room admitted us directly into the garden, which all of us declared with one voice to be the *bonne bouche*, for nowhere else are the characteristics last hinted at more strongly displayed. Having been formed at a time when the family were young, it was fitted up, as I may say, with an especial regard to their amusement, at the same time that instruction was not overlooked. At the head of the principal alley, a figure of the sun is placed; along the alley, perched on sticks, are figures of the various planets and their satellites, in such sizes, and at such intervals, as to express their relations to the sun and to each other, while the chief elements of each are stated on a tablet below. In the same line are inserted small tablets, expressing, by the distance from the head of the walk to the several points indicated, the length of the principal large vessels of modern times—the Britannia royal ship of 130 guns, the Great Western and Great Britain steamers. Here, however, the most remarkable thing is a light paling which extends along one side of the walk, bearing a continuous slip of wood, on which is painted the chronology of the world in the ratio of an inch to every year. It is wholly the work of the Major's own hands, and cost him four months to execute. As you pass along, you first catch a few sparse notices, as, "At this time men began to call on the name of the Lord"—"Methuselah born"—"Adam dies;" and so forth. Half way down the walk, you find King David reigning, and the Greeks sacking Troy. Then come the glories of Rome—the darkness of the middle ages—the Crusades; and the rise of the modern nations. At the close, under 1830 and 1831, we have, " Reform Bill introduced "—" Riots and disorder very general "— and finally, in a somewhat larger size of lettering, a sentence which no doubt sounded at the time like a knell—" Britain having attained a position of power, glory, and respectability never enjoyed by any other nation, it required a mighty effort to subvert her stability. This was effected on 7th June 1832, from which we may observe the decline of the British empire!" I trust that the ingenious chronologist will by and by add a postscript detailing the dismal events which have occurred during the ensuing period of national decay and degradation. Turning to another part of the garden, we find the ancient mill-course of the priory passing through it—a provocation to device and contrivance which such a man as Major Playfair could not have resisted. Accordingly, as the water rushes along, it is made to perform a great number of ingenious feats for the amusement of the family and the public. First, however, you see a Chinese bridge across it, with a number of tiny animals and human beings thronging over in different directions. Then come water-works, including jets, straight and spiral, dancing balls, a Barker's mill, the hydraulic ram, Archimedes' screw, wind-gauge, rain-gauge, &c., &c.—these being connected with a tall pagoda-like structure, in which a Chinese emperor swings about in obedience to every passing breeze, and a revolving wheel, fitted up with obliquely-arranged mirrors, casts reflections on every surrounding object. Then there are rockeries in all forms and dressings. Finally comes a pavilion, containing a little puppet theatre and an organ, all of which may be put in motion by a water-wheel, which can be sunk into the mill course, while, to appearance, the mechanism is driven by a man toiling at a windlass. The grotesque waltzing party here presented elicited shouts from my young people, and sent us all away in the highest good-humour. Altogether, the mixture of cleverness, humour, and rationality which we had seen at St. Leonards, made a strong impression on me, and I could not help applauding a life in which the gifts of fortune and the high privilege of leisure are to all appearance so felicitously used.

I returned from St. Andrews more than ever convinced of the immense power for good which exists in every individual of mankind. Here is one not inconsiderable bit of our common country—a town of above five thousand inhabitants—which has been in five years, as it were transmuted into something better, through the almost sole efforts of one private citizen.

May not similar phenomena be effected elsewhere? When I ask the question, I feel how unjust it is to such doings as those of Major Playfair to regard them in their material aspect, or to designate them as local. Physical in the first place, they are in the long-run moral, in as far as elegance and cleanliness are refining and ennobling influences. Through the principle of example, they are operations not merely upon one little spot of ground, but which may be expected to exercise an influence on surrounding districts, so as finally to affect the whole country. But if they did nothing else than show what one man may do by a well-directed mind for the benefit of his fellow-creatures, they would fulfil a high object, and be entitled to the public gratitude.

ANE AULD BALLAD UPON A NEW KNYCHTE.

Written by G. Mackgill, Esq. of Kemback, and sung to the air of " The Fine Old English Gentleman."

I.

The wind blaws keen at Aberdeen,
    Sae does it at Dundee,
O'er mony a stately toun it blaws,
    In Scotland's cauld countrie.
But of a' the touns the wind blaws o'er,
    There's nane sae dear to me,
As the grey towers o' St. Andrews toun,
    St. Andrews on the sea.

II.

For there, I ween, dwells Golfers keen,
    A jolly companie ;
And mony a leal and trusty friend,
    And mony a fair ladye ;
And there " the Major " keeps his state,
    And rules the auld citye ;
A mighty man of heart and hand,
    And the pynk of courtesye,
Is the Major of St. Andrews toun—St Andrews on the sea.

III.

In distant lands he led the bands
    Of India's chivalrie ;
In hot Bengal, the best of all,
    The Horse Artillerie.
With meikle credit and renown,
    He served the Companie ;
And if he served himself also,
    The more it pleaseth me ;
This Major of St. Andrews toun—St. Andrews on the sea.

IV.

And when at length, in health and strength,
    He reached his native shore,
He set himself with might and main,
    The citye to restore.
With main and might, what he thought right,
    He did it fearlesslie,
And no man dared to wag his beard,
    When told to let it be,
By this all potent tyrant of St. Andrews on the sea.

V.

The streets he paved, the wrath he braved
 Of the fishwife progenie.
The Mussel Scaup rebellion,
 He quelled with stern decree.
He made the Madras, flare up like gas,
 As a famed Academie.
And equal justice did to all
 Of high and low degree;
This Provost of St. Andrews toun—St. Andrews on the sea.

VI.

But time would fail, e'er half the tale
 I could declare to thee,
Of how he fought the Home Office,
 And banged the Treasurie.
And all for the sake of the Colleges,
 And the Universitie.
Though whether he ever got thanks for the same,
 Is quite unknown to me;
Except being told to write with his name—the letters LL.D.

VII.

The Old Town Hall, best work of all,
 He improved most sensiblie;
With a Market Place and Private Rooms,
 Most beautiful to see;
And all against the wish of those,
 Who cried out let it be,
For I won't subscribe to keep up such
 A splendid deformitie;
Although much required, and long desired,
By the Provost of St. Andrews—that toun upon the sea.

VIII.

The Queen she dwells in Windsor Tow'r,
 In Windsor Hall sits she;
Says—"Albert, call Sir George the Grey,
 And bid him bring to me
The best and worthiest of our land,
 That they may knighted be.
And first of all, let us install
 Our friend from the North Countrie;
That mirror of all Magistrates, and make him K.C.B."

IX.

"Sir Hugh, arise," the Queen she cries,
   As he knelt beside her knee;
"I wot 'twere better for all this land,
   And better far for me,
If we were served but half as well,
   By our well-paid Ministrye,
As you have served your native toun,
   Withouten fear or fee,
Sir Hugh, thou Prince of Provosts from St. Andrews on the sea."

X.

Now let us sing, long live the Queen,
   And the Provost long live he;
And here's a health to his Ladye fair,
   And a health to his Fam'lie;
And let us all, both great and small,
   Learn from this historie,
To work the work that's given us
   Upright and manfully,
Like Sir Hugh, the famous Provost of St. Andrews on the sea."

PATON AND RITCHIE, PRINTERS, EDINBURGH.

CPSIA information can be obtained at www.ICGtesting.com
Printed in the USA
LVOW02s1810110713

342481LV00016B/495/P

9 781241 690878